SHORT CRUISE ON THE *VYNER BROOKE*

CW00819618

Ralph E.H. Armstrong

Short Cruise on the *Vyner Brooke*

With a Foreword by
Countess Mountbatten of Burma

GEORGE MANN *of* MAIDSTONE

Ralph E.H. Armstrong

SHORT CRUISE ON THE *VYNER BROOKE*

© Ralph E.H. Armstrong, 2003

Foreword © Countess Mountbatten of Burma

Cover by *Bax*

First published 2003

ISBN 0 7041 0406 7

Printed and bound in the United Kingdom
and published by George Mann Books
of PO Box 22, Maidstone
in the English County of Kent

This Book is Dedicated to
the memory of
my Mother and my two Sisters

SHORT CRUISE ON THE *VYNER BROOKE*

Contents

Patricia Mountbatten,
the elder daughter of Lord and Lady Louis Mountbatten,
and now Countess Mountbatten of Burma,
as a Third Officer in the WRNS at the end of the Second World War

Foreword

by

Countess Mountbatten of Burma

Although it is well over half a century since the terrible events related in this book took place, they never can, and never should, be forgotten.

To a younger generation they may seem incredible — to the older generation (especially of course those who lived through and survived them) they will always remain a terrible, vivid example of 'man's inhumanity to man'.

The unforgettable nature of these events is borne out by the fact that it has taken nearly sixty years for Ralph Armstrong who lived through them as a boy, to record them for posterity.

The courage and determination to survive against all the odds of those who did survive is something we can all marvel at, and puts the small trials and tribulations we all have to face at times into a proper perspective.

Patricia Mountbatten of Burma

Family and friends in our Heeren Building apartment.
Paddy and Grace sixth and seventh from the left

1

Before the Onslaught

IN SINGAPORE in 1941, the war in Europe seemed so very far away and that it would never affect us at all.

It had been raging since 1939, but the closest it had come to us so far was half the world away in North Africa.

It was true that troops had been arriving by almost every ship, but this only heightened our comfortable feeling that — as we were constantly assured — we were living in an impregnable fortress. Life was quite pleasant.

Our family was living in the Heeren Building, a large block of apartments at the corner of Orchard Road and Cairnhill Road. There was my father and mother, my married sister Grace and her little boy, Marc, and my other sister, Dixie. Grace's husband was a cheerful young Irishman serving with the Royal Air Force and Dixie's boyfriend was an Englishman with an Army Signals Unit. They intended to marry, I think, but later events intervened and it was not to be.

Singapore had been founded in 1819 by Sir Thomas Stamford Raffles, and had thrived as a Free Port. There was no customs or excise duty on most imported items, which meant one could obtain goods from all over the world very cheaply, and they were certainly available in all their variety in the shops. Wonderful silks and cloths from India, China and Persia were stacked in rolls on the merchants' shelves. Ladies could pick their curtains from the best quality fabrics, and have them made up for a pittance. Following the latest fashion in dress was just a matter of choosing a pattern from a stylish magazine and giving it to a dressmaker. It would be prepared and ready for fitting in a day or two.

Most of the newsagents' shops and stalls were run by Indians. The magazines on their racks in the Orchard Road area were chiefly in the English language, from England, America, New Zealand and Australia. Fresh food, carefully inspected and health checked, was available in the large city market. One could get almost anything there and, on the odd chance that one couldn't, there was also a supermarket complete with delicatessen close-by.

Pax Britannica reigned, and my perception of it as a boy was that the administration of the country and its laws was fair and square to everyone, and very happy we were with it.

Below the generality of English Common Law and Equity, each ethnic group was allowed to have justice administered according to its own customs and religion. For instance, there were Shariah courts to deal with Islamic matters, courts to take into account things like the Hindu joint family, and others to look into matters of Chinese custom. It worked well and everyone seemed satisfied.

The harbour was full of ships from all over the world. Raffles had chosen wisely. Not only did the island have many deep-water passages, but it sat squarely on the shortest shipping route from England to East Asia. Singapore was by this time the fourth largest port in the world. Law and Order was taken so much for granted that most people were unaware that as recently as the early 1900s piracy was rampant on the high seas roundabout. In those days it would not have been prudent to take a boat trip, say, up the coast of Malaya. Even the safe passage of large vessels could not be guaranteed at that time.

Britain was slow to react but, once the ships of the Royal Navy were stationed permanently in the Far East, piracy was subdued and eventually wiped out altogether. Then came the build-up and expansion of the naval base at Seletar, on the north of the island — well sheltered in the Strait of Johore, across from the Sultan of Johore's Palace.

Somehow or other the population seemed to arrange itself into little areas. There was no compulsion. Ethnic groups just drifted in on their own. Thus there was an Indian area in the Selegie and Serangoon Roads, a Chinatown where the Chinese lived and another area where the English-speaking Straits Chinese were prominent. The Tanglin area was where the Europeans and other Westerners resided. There was also a sprinkling of Europeans in the seaside areas. The Malays, the original inhabitants, generally clung to the coastal areas in their *Kampongs*, although they also populated small inland farms. Jewish business people seemed to be predominant along Sofia Road.

My father and his brothers had come to the island in the early days, being transferred from administrative posts in Sumatra when they were no longer needed. In Singapore, I was led to believe they had good positions, such as in Main Roads, Harbour Master's Office, etc. My father himself was manager at Robinson's, which was one of the first and largest department stores in Raffles Place. He and Mr Robinson got on very well. This state of affairs continued until the late 1920s or early 1930s when Mr Robinson died and my father decided that the time had come to make a change. He left to set up his own department store and some years later Robinson's acquired a new manager in Mr L.C. Hutchings, who by his unstinting help and generosity when war came, and the city was attacked by the Japanese, made his own name and the name of his store something to be remembered with pride and with thankfulness in the dark days ahead.

As a young lad my friends were varied. There was David, son of a RAF Wing Commander, and an American boy named Steve from one of the flats on the other side of the Heeren Building. Also a German boy from nearby. There was Molly, who was English, the daughter of the owners of the large Dry Cleaners on Orchard Road and Bob, the son of the Area Head of the Watch Tower organisation, who lived in a big two-storey house on the hill. There was also another English girl named Beliesha and a Dutch family in a nearby house in Cairnhill Road, whose mother used to give us delicious cookies, so their place was a favourite for tea.

The general area where my friends lived was roughly a triangle bounded by Cairnhill Road, Bideford (pronounced Bidiford) Road, and Orchard Road. There was some vacant land with a little marshland and bushes in the centre and also vacant land on the far side of Bideford Road, so we had plenty of room to play.

15

The Heeren Building
on the corner of Orchard and Churchill Roads, Singapore.
The Armstrong apartment is on the far right, facing Churchill Road

Myself and friends
(left to right) David, Bob, the German boy
and myself

The whole of the left side of Cairnhill Road, right up to its intersection at the top with Bideford Road, had once belonged to my dad. He had sold it some years earlier for only ten cents a square foot not realising how valuable it would become in later years. He said he felt like kicking himself sometimes when he thought about it.

At our place, there was always some visitor or other. My father's friends were mostly business contacts, who made deals to provide the type of goods he would sell in his store. These contacts included one clean-cut, polished Japanese gentleman, who was dealing in canned green peas, which were quite popular in the restaurants. We learned later that quite a few of the Japanese businessmen were spies, but I don't think he was one of them. My mother's friends were mostly continental Europeans, very polite people, whilst my two sisters' visitors — husband and boyfriend and their comrades — were mostly drawn from the Forces, a good mannered and cheerful crowd.

In 1941 the Japanese occupied French Indo-China (which is now divided into Laos, Cambodia and Vietnam). This seemed to cause great concern to the adults. As children, some of us wondered what all the fuss was about. There was no television at that time and we relied on the radio for our news. The only way to see actual footage of the war was in the cinemas, from the British Movietone News or Pathé Gazette, shown before the main movie. We saw the Dunkirk evacuation in June 1940 and then the British successes against the Italians in North Africa that same year. If we had cared to look at the map we would have understood the concern of the adults, as we would have seen how really close Indo-China was to Malaya.

When the British withdrew from France at the time of Dunkirk, the French were forced to capitulate to Nazi Germany, and a new French Government — the Vichy Government — was formed under Marshal Petain, ostensibly neutral but in fact under the thumb of the Germans. This meant that the French colonies, including Indo-China, came under a regime dominated by the Axis powers. Accordingly, when pressure was applied by the Germans, France gave permission to their allies, the Japanese, to occupy northern Indo-China under the pretext of protecting it. The Japanese were established there by mid-1941.

In contrast, the Netherlands East Indies (now Indonesia), took orders from the Dutch Government-in-Exile which had moved to London after the German seizure of Holland. In the Netherlands East Indies, they even had collections for the Allied War Effort such as 'Buy a Spitfire.' This collection was so successful that it was not long before planes built with the money collected were airborne against the Germans.

Amongst the boys in my group, even our German friend, who at one time had proudly sported a metal Nazi swastika badge, began to have second thoughts about Hitler and came to the view that his regime was in the wrong.

It was an exciting time for souvenir collecting, as we accumulated all sorts of military and Air Force insignia, badges, brass buttons and even light arms. I myself had a boxful of souvenirs as well as a real sword and scabbard and a small square pistol.

My father yelled, "What are you doing with that thing, you will kill somebody if you are not careful." So I emptied out all the ammunition and kept the pistol out of sight on top of the picture rail which ran around the living room wall. The ammunition was safe in a drawer.

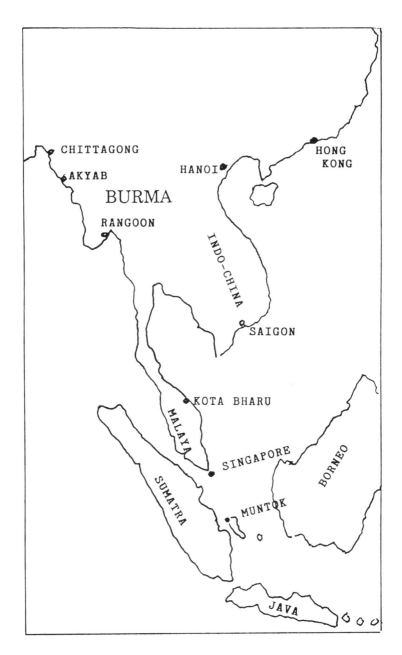

Malaya and Sumatra

2

Invasion

AT ABOUT FOUR FIFTEEN IN THE MORNING of Monday 8th December 1941, we were rudely awakened by the sound of falling bombs. We all scrambled out of bed wondering what on earth was happening. I had never woken up so early in my life. Waking up in the morning at six or six-thirty to go and see the sunrise at Bouna Vista Road was bad enough.

We all gathered in the living room to hear what the radio had to say. Our Chinese *amah* who was living in the servants' quarters promptly appeared and decided to make tea for everyone. The lights all over the city had been on all night, with even the neon signs still flashing.

There had been no warning.

At about seven Greg one of my friends popped up, all excited, saying, "The Japanese have attacked! They have even bombed Pearl Harbour and Hong Kong."

"Yes," we said, " we have heard it on the radio and for your information they have already landed at Kota Bharu." (In northern Malaya, near the Thai border).

Another lady from one of the flats upstairs came in and joined the discussion.

Subsequently we learned that there had been a widespread Japanese co-ordinated attack. Although the local times and even some dates were different they had all taken place virtually simultaneously when reckoned on Greenwich Mean Time.

Those approximate times were:

1700hrs Gmt 7th December 1941,
Kota Bharu landings, (local time 1.00am, 8th December)

1830hrs Gmt 7th December
Pearl Harbour (local time 8.00am, 7th December)

2100hrs Gmt 7th December
Singapore bombed, (local time 4.15am, 8th December)

2330hrs Gmt 7th December
Hong Kong bombed, (local time 8am, 8th December)

2230hrs Gmt 7th December
Manila bombed, (local time 9.30am, 8th December)

At *1830hrs Gmt 7th December,* Japanese troops crossed the Thai border and reached the outskirts of Bangkok on 9th December. In Shanghai, Japanese forces simply crossed over from the Japanese sector of the city and occupied all of the other sectors.

At Kota Bharu, the Japanese seaborne invaders had difficulty landing due to the heavy surf and then encountered stiff resistance in the town, but they landed almost unopposed on the narrow strip of land which joins Malaya and Thailand, just north of Kota Bharu, and took the towns of Singora and Petani at 2am local time 8th December (Gmt 18.30 7th December), about one hour after occupying Kota Bharu. The U.S. Wake Island was bombed that same day, destroying about twelve aircraft on the ground and two Japanese destroyers shelled the U.S. island of Midway.

U.S. forces in the Philippines were warned by radio from Hawaii that a bombing raid could be imminent and all aircraft were ordered into the air to escape being destroyed on the ground. However, the Japanese aerial armada was delayed taking off from Formosa by thick fog and got airborne an hour late, by which time all the American planes had been forced to land to refuel and most of them were destroyed on the ground that first day, when the armada finally struck.

RAF Spitfires were also bombed and wrecked while still on the ground in Singapore because of inadequate warning. After that, Air Raid Precautions, both civil and military, were taken more seriously.

Leaflets were distributed advising the population to tape

up windows in criss-cross fashion to reduce the risk of serious injury from flying shards of glass if bombs dropped nearby. We had large windows in our apartment, so there was a fair bit of taping to be done. Lights were also to be put out or dimmed if the air raid sirens sounded. Volunteers — men and women with ARP armbands — patrolled the streets. People were advised to take their own air raid precautions by sheltering under a sturdy kitchen table or other safe place while an air raid continued.

The Japanese air raids on Singapore occurred regularly at the most annoying time — which I suppose was the intention — between four and half-past four in the morning just when one was most deeply asleep. The passage between the living room and the bedrooms in our apartment was quite broad, and the ceiling was high. Walls and ceiling were solid concrete. So we placed a stout table in the passage at night to serve as an air raid shelter of sorts, but we needn't have bothered.

I do not know whether or not the word 'Heeren' in Heeren Building was connected with the 'Seventeen Heeren of the Netherlands', who traded in the Indies, but whoever had designed it had certainly made it solid to the point of overkill. Interior pillars were stout, about two feet thick. The outer walls and all the internal walls were thick and solid as well.

On one occasion, bombs did fall nearby and a Chinese man was killed close to the front of the building. The seventy-five pound bombs which the Japanese dropped, and which wrecked the old two storey shophouses in Chinatown, barely made a dent on the Heeren Building.

In the early part of December 1941, it was still possible to get about quite safely and easily. One could, for example, go to the Seaview Hotel for tiffin or have an afternoon on the beach or, as my sisters did, go to a Dinner Dance at the Adelphi Hotel in the evening. However as the Japanese advanced through Malaya the air-raids became more frequent, and one could be caught out in the open at any time, so it became less attractive to leave home.

Shopping still had to be done, of course, but there were

plenty of shops nearby in Orchard Road, not to mention dad's own store, so that was not a problem.

My mother's visitors were at our place one day discussing the atrocities committed by the Japanese invading Hong Kong with two middle aged ladies, Mrs Braun and Mrs Siekberg, and a young lady called Violet who was fond of small children. Violet spoke with a bit of a French accent, and Grace's son Marc (then about three) took to her. She in turn made much of him. All the men had been called up for active service so we didn't see as much of them as we did of their wives. Soon it was nearly Christmas.

The Japanese had moved down the peninsular swiftly. On 8th December they took Singora and Kota Bharu; on the 12th, Kanga and Alor Star; on the 15th, Kroh and Guran and on the 16th December, Penang.

We had Christmas at home for just the family and I think one friend. My mother made a dumpling dish, which she called *Schnudel*, to go with the stuffed turkey from the Cold Storage supermarket nearby. For presents I got books — *Pears Cyclopaedia*, *The Boys Own Annual* and another Annual. Amongst his other presents, baby Marc got a large teddy bear.

Our Christmas Tree had small lighted candles on it. My mother's favourite carol was *Silent Night*. When the little candles were lit in the evening and the record of *Silent Night* played in the almost blacked-out room, it had a memorable, ethereal effect.

We didn't know it at the time, but on Christmas Day 1941 our newly designated Commander-in-Chief of ABDA (American, British, Dutch and Australian) forces in South-East Asia very nearly fell into Japanese hands.

Field Marshal Sir Archibald Wavell, of Middle East fame was flying back to India, after a tour of his new command, of which — throughout the whole of the war in the Far East — Burma formed a most important part.

Generalissimo Chiang Kai Shek, the Chinese Nationalist leader, had been fighting the Japanese ever since they invaded his country in the early thirties and the Americans, who regarded him as an ally, had done their best to keep him supplied with arms and had even turned a blind eye to American subjects flying as Fighter Pilots for him in the renowned 'Tiger Squadron'. The most convenient route for war materiel into China was by land across Burma — the 'Burma Road' — and for China's survival it was vital that it was kept open. It ran from the railhead at Lashio, near Mandalay, in eastern Burma, to Kunming and Chungquin in China, a total distance of 1,381 miles, and before Japan's attack on the British Empire, a craven Imperial Government in Whitehall had given in to Tokyo's demands that it should be closed. Happily, it was then only closed for three months. Now open again, the Road was an important part of Wavell's concerns, as was Burma itself, at that time supposedly protected by a hotchpotch of individual National military units.

Some were from the Indian Army, others were troops under American General 'Vinegar Joe' Stilwell's command and some were native Burmese forces. The plane which was to carry Wavell to India had Chinese markings and was manned by Americans. The American pilot became confused by bad weather and the Field Marshal felt they were heading in the wrong direction — towards Bangkok in Thailand instead of towards India.

As Bangkok was already in Japanese hands, Wavell didn't really want to land there, so he persuaded the pilot to turn the plane around and they finally came to a town and an airstrip which the American thought was in India. Actually it turned out to be Moulmein, in Burma.

As they approached to make their landing, they were nearly shot down by the airfield defences, but then the Chinese markings on the aircraft were spotted and the gunners held their fire.

When the plane landed and Wavell stepped out, those on the ground were amazed to see their newly designated Commander-in-Chief. Arrangements were speedily made to transfer him to another plane and send him safely on his way to India. It was not a moment too soon, for the next day the

25

Japanese started bombing Burmese airfields and cities.

One morning there was a knock at the front door. My mother opened it. "Good morning, Mrs Armstrong." "Good morning, boys." Two of my friends had arrived. My mum called out, "Your friends are here."

I was just setting up my Hornby train set. They wanted to go and see a movie at the Pavilion Cinema in Orchard Road. I agreed that that was a good idea.

One of them looked at my train set-up and said, "You can't put an open wagon behind the engine." I said, "Why not?"

"Only rail cars go behind the engine," he retorted.

I said, "You idiot, this might be a goods train."

"Only a nincompoop would do that."

"You are a twerp."

"You're a twit."

"How would you like to get your block knocked off."

"Yeah, you and who else."

"Me and me alone."

"Well are we going to the pictures then?"

"Mum, is it all right if we go to the Pavilion Cinema for the matinee show? There is quite a good picture on."

My mother was worried about the bombing, but the cinema was nearby and besides, we said, the Japanese planes usually only bombed in the early morning.

"Oh, all right then, but take care, and come straight back, — no wandering around."

"Yes, mum."

So off we went.

The cinema was cool inside and at half time we bought sugar coated roasted peanuts from an Indian vendor — four cents for a small packet. Iced drinks from the soda fountain were only five cents a small glass.

The *lingua franca* for most local shopping was bazaar Malay, but the Indian soda fountain stallholder was picking up a bit of English. On a previous occasion when he had asked us whether we wanted icicles in our drinks, we had corrected him, saying they were ice cubes. This time he asked if we wanted cubicles in our drinks. We said, "They are cubes, not cubicles. Cubicles are small rooms." "Oh, sorry, sir," was his reply, "Please pardon my abysmal ignorance."

We got our drinks and went back to our seats remarking to ourselves, "Isn't it funny, he knows a big word like abysmal, but doesn't know the difference between a cube and a cubicle!"

I can't remember the name of the picture, but this was the last movie I saw before the Japanese arrived.

One day towards the end of December 1941, or early January 1942, a truck pulled up outside our building. In it was Paddy, Grace's husband. I shouted, "Paddy's here," and Grace and Marc rushed out to greet him. He could only stay that one night, and in the morning, at breakfast, told us that the truck was loaded with money. We said, "What?" so he took us outside to show us.

He lifted up the tarpaulin covering the back of the truck and, sure enough, it was stacked from top to bottom with neatly taped packets of ten-dollar notes. Mum said, "You could have been robbed during the night!" He answered, "No I couldn't, the truck was parked right outside my bedroom window, and if anyone had tried anything, I would have blasted his head off."

He had to get the truck into the city. Before leaving he told us that he had been made a Flight Sergeant and had been given flying lessons as there was a shortage of pilots and that he might be posted to Palembang, in Sumatra, as the Squadron was operating out of there now, in order to avoid being strafed on the ground. They flew across to Singapore and Malaya to engage the enemy as needed.

On 28th December 1941, Ipoh fell. The Japanese were then advancing towards the Slim River. We got news over the radio that children need not report to school in Singapore in the New Year, as the schools were not going to re-open until further notice.

On the 2nd of January 1942 the Japanese took Kampar.

By the 10th January they had reached Port Swettenham. There was no actual battle for Kuala Lumpur as such. About this time the new Commander-in-Chief of ABDA, Field

Marshal Sir Archibald Wavell made a quick appraisal of the situation confronting his forces. Finding the troops exhausted and partly demoralized, he ordered a withdrawal to a new line extending from Muar across and up to the vicinity of Segamat. This was done quickly and effectively, and in the newspapers referred to as 'Withdrawal according to plan'. Consequently Kuala Lumpur escaped the worst and was practically unscathed.

My mother was the kindest, gentlest person I have ever known. If she could say something good about a person, she would. If not, she preferred not to say anything at all. She always tried to see the best in people. There was no malice in her. My father was always busy, and did not have much time to spare. While I was waiting impatiently for an answer to a question, he would say, "Don't fidget, boy."

Of my two sisters, Dixie was the more reserved in nature. I would not go so far as to say she was prim and proper, but her nature and inclinations generally lay in that direction. Grace, on the other hand, was vivacious and fun loving. Like all young girls before her marriage, she had many boyfriends and when they went out to the seaside, lunches or movies I was usually told to go along with them. Open coupé cars were the fashion at that time, and I would sit in the back seat.

If my mother thought I had a cheerful disposition in my own way, she was ten times more so than I. No matter what she did, in my eyes she could do no wrong. At the christening of baby Marc it was decided to give him half a dozen names so that he could make a choice for himself, later in life. The family agreed to abide by his choice. The name Marc is not the original name he was known by. It is his second name, and this is the one he chose.

3
Reinforcements

ALTHOUGH WE WERE NOT GIVEN THE DETAILS, we heard that the island's garrison was being substantially reinforced. What was actually happening was that the 18th Indian Division and some Hurricane fighters were on the way. Unfortunately, six fast landing craft that had arrived from America were destroyed by the Japanese on January 1st.

Dutch reinforcements *en route* to Malaya, December 1941
Photo courtesy of Netherlands Institute for War Documentation

The advance troops of the Indian Division (the 45th Brigade) arrived in Singapore around mid-January together with fifty new Hurricane fighters.

Another ninety Hurricane fighters were due by the end of February 1942 on the *Athene* and *Indomitable.* Protection of these vessels involved utilising most of the naval forces in Singapore except small craft which were being used to protect shipping entering and leaving the harbour. Most of the remaining fighter aircraft were also deployed on protecting shipping and supplies, which left troops fighting the Japanese with hardly any air support. These were difficult choices for those who allocated resources. But all but one of the supply ships got through safely.

The exception was the *Empress of Asia*, sunk on the 5th February 1942.

All through the battles on the Malay Peninsula, the defending troops fought valiantly, from the battles involving the Punjab and Gurkha Regiments and the 1st Leicesters (who bore the main brunt of the first attack), to the action at Slim River where the Argyll and Sutherland Highlanders faced the invaders together with the Gurkha and Punjab Regiments.

But the battle which really caught my imagination was the Australian action at Gemas and later along the Muar Road.

The 8th Australian Division commanded by Major General Gordon Bennett comprised two Brigades, the 22nd and 27th and the 2/4 Machine Gun Unit, plus support troops. The 22nd arrived in February 1941 and the 27th in August 1941 and Major General Gordon Bennett gave them training in jungle warfare.

All along the Malay Peninsula the rapid Japanese advance had been assisted by their use of cheap Japanese bicycles. Thus, while our troops had to go the distance on foot, the Japanese were much more mobile, cycling along the good roads. If attacked, the Japanese just threw their bicycles into the bushes by the roadside and when the attack was over, formed up again.

By the time they got to Gemas in mid January 1942, the Allies had become aware of this tactic. It was around this time that the Australian 28th Infantry Brigade was sent to Gemas from Mersing on the east coast where they had established positions against a possible coastal advance. The Australians were bored, waiting behind the well-fortified defences of Mersing (which the Japanese did not attack) and eager to see some action. The Australian 27th Infantry Brigade (Brigadier D.C. Maxwell) started moving up to Gemas where the fatigued 9th Indian Division was holding on.

The newly arrived 45th Indian Infantry Brigade was sent up to relieve, and the 9th Division was allowed to fall back to take a well earned rest. The 30th Battalion under Colonel Gallaghan took up positions near a bridge, which had been laced with explosives, ready for detonation, and waited. They did not have to wait long. Within forty-eight hours, chatting and laughing, the Japanese came down the track on bicycles towards the bridge. The Australians had strict orders to hold their fire until the signal was given.

After several hundred Japanese had crossed over the bridge and the Australians on both sides of the road could hardly contain themselves any longer, there was a sudden blast. The bridge had gone up, and the order came, 'Fire!' The Australians on both sides of the road opened fire and lobbed in hand grenades. The road was littered with dead bodies. This was one place the 'cycle down the road tactic' certainly did not work.

At another location, the Japanese were approaching in quite large numbers, calling out, "Don't shoot, we are Indians." The Australian Captain spoke to headquarters on the landline, and it so happened that Brigadier Maxwell was there. He replied, "There are no Indian troops in that area." The Australians charged out with bayonets fixed and once again the Japanese attack became a debacle.

Dutch bombers, protected by Australian fighter planes, flew overhead and bombed and strafed the Japanese motor transports that were following. Further out along the Muar Road, anti-tank guns took up positions on both sides of the road facing the expected oncoming Japanese tanks. They came straight through and the anti-tank gunners opened fire. About nine Japanese tanks were put out of action.

News of these successes got through to Johore Bahru and Singapore, by word of mouth as well as from short reports in the newspapers and on the radio. It was very heartening.

However, great as these engagements on the main roads were, jungle-trained Empire troops were insufficient to halt the advance of the enemy through the jungle all of the time. The Japanese managed to get round to the rear of the defenders. Suddenly having the enemy behind them as well as in front upset the Indians more than the Australians.

At Mersing, the Japanese did the same thing. Ignoring the prepared defences facing north, they made their way through the jungle to attack the defence positions from the rear. In Churchill's six-volume account of World War II he said he was amazed that the defending forces did not cover their rear. He said it was one of the basic principles of defence established as far back as Plevna, whatever that was — clearly as unknown to Singapore's defence chiefs as it is to me.

Churchill said that he no more thought of a fortress not being defended from the rear, than a ship being launched without a bottom. He had expected that a ring of detached self-sustainable fortresses would be built on the north side of the island, but this was not done.

Who was to blame? At this late juncture, who knows?

Mersing, on the east coast, was taken by the Japanese on January 26th 1942 and three days later, on January 29th Kluang in central Johore.

By January 31st 1942 the Japanese were in Johore Bahru, at the southernmost tip of the Malay Peninsula, facing Singapore across the narrow straits.

Churchill's insistence that there should have been a circle of detached little forts to protect the landward side was indeed a good idea, but it could not be implemented now.

For us, the first week of February 1942 became somewhat more unnerving than all that had gone before. Whereas until now we had had air raids preceded by siren warnings, there was now the added danger of shells, which would come over at any time.

The only warning one got was the high-pitched whine of

the shell approaching. This gave you about three seconds flat to duck for cover.

The next thing was the arrival of the Japanese on the north side of the Island of Singapore itself. The first landings did not come across at the narrowest point of the Johore Strait at the north east as expected, but west of the Naval Base. There were a number of notable battles on the way down, and one place that held very well was at Bouna Vista, defended by the Malay Regiment and a newly arrived Australian unit.

While they were holding this position, stragglers from other units were drifting past them — heading listlessly towards Singapore city. The Australians wondered what the Malay Regiment must have thought, seeing this, but nothing was said.

The Australians said they would never forget the quiet and confident way in which the Malays stood firm and cheerfully carried out their tasks. Strangely, in spite of all this, many of the European inhabitants of Singapore did not seem to be unduly worried by the prospect of Japanese occupation, as they expected this to be brief. They would regret this attitude later and the Chinese, who had always known better, suffered terribly.

Singapore's greatest problem was with its water supply. The bulk of the city's water came from the Kota Tinggi region in Johore. The water held in Singapore's own reservoirs, although large, could only sustain the population's requirements for a limited time, unless there was continuous heavy monsoon rain.

The Japanese were in fact, carrying out a bluff. They had extended their supply lines too far and were becoming short of the warlike materiel they needed. They had less than half the forces we had on the island. However they now had control of Singapore's water supply.

In hindsight it is easy to see how impossible it would have been to continue the battle on Singapore Island if the water supply had run out. What blind panic would have seized the population! Chaos would have followed. It was unthinkable.

Even if Churchill's circle of little fortresses had been built on the northside of the island, they would have had to include the defence of Kota Tinggi at all costs, otherwise that strategy, too, would have failed from shortage of water.

So in the first week of February we were told to get ready to evacuate the island. Arrangements were being made to get the Allied women and children away. By this time the fighting was getting very near to the Tanglin area. On Cairnhill Road, just five hundred yards from our home, there was a lone Japanese sniper in a tree, taking pot shots at whoever took his fancy.

There were by now little groups of troops drifting around, from time to time taking shelter in the passageways and stairwells of the buildings. One such party was right outside our front door. We said to the English corporal, "There is a Japanese sniper up the road." He answered, "Where? Where is he?" We pointed to the trees at the corner where Cairnhill Road takes a bend. The corporal said, "We'll fix him," and all seven of them went up the road, keeping to the sides as they went.

Whether they got the sniper or not, we did not know, because they did not return. The next time we looked out there were Indian troops in the stairwell instead. After a while they, too, moved on.

4

The *Vyner Brooke*

ON THURSDAY 12TH FEBRUARY 1942 we had to report for evacuation.

In the early 1930s there was a song about a Russian called Ivan Skavinski Skavar fighting an Egyptian Arab called Abdul Abulbul Emir. As we started heading out from the Heeren Building I could hear this record playing somewhere. We said our farewells to Dad and got all our bags into a taxi which was waiting outside for us. We heard that the sniper in the tree in Cairnhill Road had been shot down. The Japanese were said to be already advancing down Bukit Timah Road. By this time there was quite a bit of shelling, and smoke everywhere, but the Malay taxi driver chatted on as usual, stopping at all the red lights, seemingly without a care in the world. Some shops also were open as usual.

We were told to report to the HMS *Laburnum* at the wharves. It turned out to be a land station by that name. When we arrived, there was already quite a crowd milling about. We were allotted to the SS *Vyner Brooke*. To my eyes, as she stood off-shore, she looked lovely. The nicest looking ship of the lot. She looked like a well-built, sturdy ship, with a style of her own. She had been requisitioned and painted grey, and provided with some small deck guns.

A large launch carried us across choppy seas to our ship. Looking back at the city, with the wind and spray in my face, I saw the whole of Singapore covered by such a heavy pall of black smoke that I thought nothing would be left. When we finally got to the side of the vessel, big metal doors opened and there were cheerful English sailors on each side to help pull us and our bags into the ship, while the launch still bobbed up and down.

We found ourselves in a large room with a raised platform in the centre, where many of the evacuees had settled down. Apparently, we were heading for Australia with our baggage.

It was a relief to get away from the screeching of the shells. Among the other vessels were the *Mata Hari*, *Giang Bee* and *Li Woh*.

We learned that our Commander was Lt. R.E. Burton, RNR and that the ship was fairly fast, having been a small passenger vessel owned by the Sarawak Steamship Company plying between Sumatra, Singapore and Sarawak. She was named after the White Rajah of Sarawak, Sir Charles Vyner Brooke.

If we were expecting a grand dinner, such as we received on the ship coming out from Europe, we were disappointed. In fact there was so little to go around that we were glad we still had some food of our own.

Going out on deck we saw that the sky was dark and overcast with cloud and smoke. Fires were burning all along Singapore waterfront and the familiar buildings on Collyer Quay could no longer be clearly seen.

All of a sudden there was a cheerful sound. The Australian nurses were singing *Waltzing Matilda*. They were a noticeable group, in their smart grey uniforms.

The ship did not start moving until sundown. We heard that an Allied submarine was to be our escort and lead us out of the harbour, but we could not see it. The ship moved slowly and carefully and, as we were leaving, we heard all the noise of battle from the city and saw the black clouds and huge fires behind us. What a relief!

We went back to our place. There was no cabin for us, so we had to sleep on the deck on quilts or similar, but we did not mind as the ship had got safely out of port and into the open sea. We were away from the bombing and shelling, and slept like logs.

In the morning, going to the toilet was a bit of a problem as there were over three hundred people on the ship and there were long queues.

When we looked out we observed that we were stationary between picturesque islands. The water looked clean and inviting for a swim and the beach looked stunning, but we had to remain on the ship.

I wandered around a little, but could not find anyone of my own age that I knew. Some of the ladies were talking about their experiences which were interesting, but otherwise the day passed slowly. Some kind soul gave us a set of Ludo and we had a few games with little Marc joining in.

We moved again at night. In the morning we were once more stationary between islands, but shortly afterwards started moving again as the Captain was concerned about the Japanese activity in our area. The date was 14th February 1942, St Valentine's Day. The ship was heading towards a strait between two islands when the siren sounded. We had previously had practice drills — and different sounds translated to different things. This one meant 'Put Life Jackets on.' These were composed of six-inch cork squares, each about two inches thick sewn into khaki jackets which slipped on easily, then tied in the front.

At about 2pm the ship speeded up and started zigzagging. The air raid signal sounded. We were under attack from about half a dozen Japanese bombers. By the Captain's evasive action over twenty of the bombs missed but then one hit, and then another. One landed directly above where we were, blowing away the deck above us and leaving a gaping big fifteen foot opening. My first thought was, 'This is a problem. How are we going to sleep tonight?' It did not strike me at first that the ship would sink. 'What will happen if it rains?' I thought. I then looked over and saw that one of the ladies we had been talking to had been hit by shrapnel, and was lying in a crumpled heap — dead. She was a White Russian, I think.

It was a sight that stopped me and brought me to my senses. The only other time I had seen someone killed had been when bombs fell near the Heeren Building, in Singapore. I had ridden my bike on the balcony to the front of the building, and there was a dead Chinese man with injuries to his stomach lying there. I remember I vomited at the gruesome sight.

All of a sudden we heard the 'Abandon Ship' siren. A Ship's Officer in his smartly pressed white uniform was at the top of the stairs telling us to come up slowly and not to panic.

We got out and on to one of the upper decks — but the Japanese were still attacking. They came back with machine-guns blazing. Everybody threw themselves on the deck. some on top of each other. Standing on the upper side deck, I saw the bombs drop about fifty to a hundred yards out in the sea. The water spurted upwards like a gigantic waterspout. Someone shouted, "Get in, or you will be hit by shrapnel!"

We had to wait until the planes finally went. Then the calls came to get down the rope ladders to the lifeboats some fifteen feet below. I seem to recall, George Day, who had been our swimming instructor at St Andrews in Singapore being one of the ship's officers, guiding us down.

Another man, Eric, was a great strength and a tremendous source of assistance to us all. He saved many lives by releasing the life rafts. Yet he was abused by some of the women he was attempting to help. They accused him of trying to look up their skirts!

When we finally all settled into a big lifeboat, we encountered another difficulty. The two lifeboats to the right of us and to the left of us pulled away, but our lifeboat which was in the middle was stuck. For some reason, ours could not get away from the side of the ship which now started creaking, crake craake craake, crake craake craake, like a tree about to fall. We looked up and saw that it was starting to come down on top of us.

There was a shout, "Abandon lifeboat. Jump — jump quickly," and we all had to jump into the water and get clear. I swam away blindly, not really knowing where I was heading, but trying to stay near our family. The lifejackets were good; it was almost impossible to sink.

All of a sudden life rafts were bobbing about all around us. We reached one and scrambled on. Two or three of our family were on one raft, and the others on another raft nearby.

The raft I was on was actually two rafts stuck one on top of the other with a bit of the bottom edge of the one underneath jutting out like a ledge.

Also on our raft was June Bourhill, the nine-year-old

daughter of an English Singapore Municipal Council Officer, a White Russian young lady and a badly burned Malay seaman from the engine room. It seemed one of the bombs had exploded there.

Paddling furiously, we tried to push the two rafts together so that we could get all our family on one of them. While we were doing this, a sudden wave smashed the two rafts alongside each other. June Bourhill, who had been holding on over the edge of our raft had a finger chopped off at the top knuckle. It happened in an instant. She screamed and rushed over to me, clinging to me with her head on my lap and sobbing. There she stayed for the three days and nights we were at sea.

We managed to get all our family onto one raft, which had ropes cleated around the edge which we could hold on to. My mother and my sisters Grace and Dixie tore off part of their white petticoats to try and bandage the Malay seaman who was suffering terribly. We had repeatedly been warned never to drink the salt seawater as it would drive one mad and we stuck to that rule — no matter what. But the Malay, I suppose due to his burns, kept on drinking the salt water. He would not listen to our advice. It seems that what we had been told was correct because, by his mumbling, the Malay gave us the impression that he intended to end it all. He suddenly stood up and said, "I'm going."

Mum said, "Save him, stop him quick!"

Mum happened to be holding the baby and, in my case, June was still in some pain, although she had quietened down a little. That left Grace, Dix and the White Russian lady. However it was not easy to even try to touch him, let alone grab him, as his skin was raw from the burns he had suffered from the explosion in the Engine Room.

The ladies did not know how to hold him and physically they were no match for him. In his state of mind, he might have dragged them over with him. All we could do was watch, transfixed, as he walked off the edge, and into the sea, where he disappeared. A merciful end, I suppose.

We could see the land in the distance on both sides

because we were in a strait. Having read the *Boy's Own* adventure weeklies, I fully expected rescue vessels to come speeding out to save us. But this was not Singapore. There were no rescue vessels — nothing.

When nightfall came we had to keep prodding each other to keep awake, to make sure we did not fall off the raft, as we were all sitting around the edge with our feet dangling in the water. Wailing sounds and cries seemed to come to us from the distance. As each wave struck we were drenched. In the calm periods it was all right — but otherwise we were left shivering.

I don't know why sharks did not attack us. Maybe they were frightened off by the bombing.

It was pitch dark at times, but at other times it lightened up and one could see a lighthouse flashing in the distance. When the dawn came, it was lovely, and we were able to dry out. The water achieved a pleasant temperature and we could have been down at the seaside for a picnic if it were not for the fact that we were absolutely starving and without even a drop of water to drink.

Having to keep awake all the time was the worst. As the day moved on there was blistering heat, with no shade. We started exploring the raft and found a water bottle, but unfortunately it was broken. We found an oblong piece of canvas, but did not know what to do with it. Later we learned that it was to catch rainwater in.

At first relieving ourselves was a problem. We all had to turn our backs and not look. After the second day, because we were neither eating nor drinking, the necessity did not arise.

We paddled hard to try and push the raft to land, but no matter how hard we paddled, we could not get any nearer. The strong currents seemed to drive us away relentlessly. Dixie said, "How lucky the people in the lifeboats are, they must have reached shore and been given nice warm beds."

Little did we know that one of the lifeboats which had been alongside ours had carried some of the Australian nurses who had met an unfortunate end. It seems that when they reached Radji beach on Bangka Island near the town of

Muntok they were made to walk down into the sea and machinegunned by the Japanese.

Their cruel end is recorded in *Knights of Bushido* by Lord Russell of Liverpool, a comprehensive record of Japanese wartime atrocities.

5

The Swamp

ON THE RAFT ON THE SECOND DAY, we started getting weaker. Marc was only three years old, still little more than an infant. Grace was distraught because there was not even a drop of milk to give him. She pricked her finger with a safety pin to give him a little blood. Thinking back now I don't know whether that was such a good idea.

When circumstances are such that you are completely helpless, when there is no one to turn to and nothing more you can do on your own, even the most hardened agnostic turns to God. We were neither agnostics nor atheists, just not very practising. We prayed, and asked to be delivered.

By the third day we were well and truly disorientated. We were shivering at night, blistered in the day, and groggy from lack of sleep. We did not even know whether we could get through the third night but somehow or other we did.

Mercifully, on the fourth morning, we found we had drifted near land. Mum said, "Look there are men moving around on the beach." We could see no men. At that time we thought she must have been hallucinating.

However, many years after the war, I learned that there were others in another boat who'd had the same experience, at approximately the same place. In their case the vision they saw through the mist in front of them actually turned up in reality, but some miles further on — so there must have been some refraction in the atmosphere at that spot.

Although there were seven men in their boat, they too had to fight against the currents in the Bangka Strait which seemed diabolically determined to prevent them reaching the haven of the land.

The bay we were approaching looked like a normal beach — the same sweeping curve, albeit on a somewhat smaller scale. We paddled frantically to try to get to it. Mum still said she thought she saw men running around. We got to shore and scrambled through the shallows. I fully expected to see a road a few yards in from the beach, but there was only swamp. Mud, more mud, more swamp. We saw a lighthouse in the distance (back the way we had come), so we started walking in that direction, which turned out to be north. We kept as close to the ocean as we could, but still could not avoid the mud. Every few steps we took, our shoes got stuck in it. We had to retrieve them. Eventually we gave up on the shoes and sloshed along barefoot.

Under the mud there was a strange sort of shoot sprouting up. Something like an asparagus spear, but a bit stiffer — about three or four inches high and half to three-quarters of an inch thick. They were everywhere. Stepping on them scratched our bare feet leaving them raw and smarting, one more thing to add to our catalogue of other cuts, abrasions, bruises and blisters. Although we somehow stumbled along all day, the lighthouse did not seem to get any closer.

Eventually we reached a twenty-foot patch of higher ground (about three feet above the swamp). It was late, nearly nightfall. We all gathered leaves and grasses — anything to make something soft to lie on. As darkness fell we imagined shapes in the trees and bushes. Someone said, "I think I see an orang-utan in that tree." But we were too tired and couldn't care less. For the first time in days the seven of us slept right through the night.

In the morning, when we awoke, we found we were covered with tiny crabs trying to bite us. When we moved they ran away, but we were badly scratched, lacerated and sunburned. Shortly after, someone said, "There is a fishing boat coming." I thought it must be another hallucination, but when I looked up I saw there was indeed a large sampan being rowed in to shore by the two men in it. They came to within about ten to fifteen feet of us but would not come any closer.

We asked them to help, but they said they were afraid that a Japanese aeroplane would see them. We tried to convince them not to worry — there were no planes around. Eventually, Grace took off her wedding ring and stretched out her hand to offer it to them. They then came in to shore, tied up the boat, took the ring, and said they would take us to a place to hide. One of the men appeared to be about fifty years of age and the other man twenty or under. The younger man was told to lead us to the place. He said, "Follow me" and started walking towards a jungle path. He was taking us back the way we had come, but on firm ground. He knew where the pathway was. We were so weak — we could hardly walk, and kept stumbling and falling down. He was impatient, telling us 'Lakas, lakas — hurry up!'

Grace said that it was wonderful that her wedding ring had saved us all. Eventually we got to a place where there was a creek, with shallow sluggish water and where lay an abandoned, partly wrecked, motor launch. I remember that the interior cabin was still fully decked and we were all able to get into it. Our guide left us there and we simply flopped down exhausted.

The two men came back later with a huge container of water, and a massive pot of rice with some fried *ikan bilis* — tiny little fish like anchovies. Even though we had starved for three days, we could not eat much more than one spoonful of rice, but we drank copious amounts of water.

The seven of us huddled together and fell asleep again on the planks. When evening came, there were literally not hundreds but thousands of mosquitoes. One could slap or kill as many as one wanted, but they still kept coming. Only exhaustion allowed us to sleep while we fed the whole mangrove mosquito population with our blood.

The next day, or it could have been two days later, a Dutchman in Navy whites appeared. The Malay fishermen accompanied him. He had arrived in command of a very large lifeboat, but it was already full of people and could not take even one more, let alone seven. The Dutchman gave us tinned provisions, such as potatoes and corned beef, and he strictly ordered the Malays to look after us and not let us be harmed, otherwise he would deal with them severely after the war ended and the Dutch came back. We could see his lifeboat and the people in it anchored not far offshore and we could see how crowded it was. He wished us luck, said good-bye and headed off in the direction of Batavia, as Jakarta was then known.

Following this, I don't know how many days later, since I lost track of time, the two natives said they would take us to Bangka Island, which we could see in the distance, though we knew that it was not as close as it looked. We were not familiar with the name and wondered if, somehow or other, we had got to Siam. "Is it Bangkok?" we asked.

They said: "No, Bangka."

"Do you know where Bangkok is?" my mother asked.

"Yes," the older man said, "it is in See-Aam."

We gathered that they knew. So this island we were looking at across the sea had to be another place. They said they would take us first to their *kelong*, their house on stilts in the sea, and from there across to the island.

6
House on the Sea

THANKFUL FOR THE OPPORTUNITY to get out of the swamp we all got into the sampans and the two men rowed us across the sea to their *kelong*. We climbed up the stairs and came up on decking on one side where they salted and dried the fish that they caught.

Their womenfolk came out to greet us. They were neatly dressed with only light head coverings of flimsy scarves, or no head coverings at all.

They had a meal prepared for us and there were clean woven mats on the floor with places for us to sit around and eat. The room was cool and we could smell the aroma of the freshly cooked dishes. The rice was fluffy and steam was still coming from the dish as they brought it out of the kitchen. What a contrast to the cold clammy stuff we had been getting until now.

It was quite a simple meal of rice, saltfish, *Kang Kong* (a local vegetable, rich in iron like spinach) and *sambals*, with pieces of *Tow Hoo* (Bean Curd). Something like a Singapore stallholder's meal called *Nasi Lemak*. We found it delicious. I suppose anything would have been delicious to us at that time, but this was really well prepared.

My sketch of The House on the Sea

They collected and stored rainwater in forty-four gallon drums as it ran off the roof and since the rainfall was heavy in this region —almost a deluge every three or four days — there was no fresh-water shortage.

They had two or three rooms in the place. It was more spacious than it looked. The seven of us — that is Mum, Grace, Dixie, June Bourhill, the White Russian lady, Marc and I — were allotted the centre room.

The White Russian lady may well have been living in the same block as us in the Heeren Building in Singapore, but in one of the upstairs apartments.

The flooring was made of bamboo or cane slats, and upon this they laid their mats. It was clean; the whole place was cool and quite pleasant.

If one lifted the mat one could see the sea through the slats underneath. The mosquito population was minimal, so sleep that night was heaven.

The place we were in was in the Strait of Bangka — near to the Sumatra coast.

The days passed by and the fishermen made no move to get us to Bangka Island, as the Dutchman had insisted they should. Instead, we caught snatches of their conversation in the next room — "I think I'll take that one as an extra wife . ." (Muslims are allowed four). It was the older one speaking, and the younger replied, "I fancy a young one . . " My mother and sisters and the others became concerned as they could understand enough of the Malay language, and they started really pestering the fishermen to get us across to the island.

In their turn the Malays kept making excuses about the weather not being right, or there being no moon. But the womenfolk were very edgy now and supporting us were the fishermen's own women for obvious reasons. We reminded them of the dire consequences threatened by the Dutchman if we were not moved as arranged.

After much haggling, and the 'gift' of another gold ring, they finally decided when we would make the trip. They did not want to leave in daylight because they thought the Japanese could see them from the sky.

The day came. We thanked the Malay women, and said good-bye and descended the wooden stairs to a large sampan. We headed off as the sun was setting with much grumbling by the two men about the weather being doubtful. As it turned out they were right. The boat ran with a small sail at first, but as we progressed we hit rain, and squalls. The boat started taking in water and we all had to bail frantically, while shivering in the rain and high winds. We wondered whether we were ever going to make it to Kobe, our destination, a small town towards the south of Bangka Island.

Eventually the morning dawned and, while still some distance from our intended landfall, we could see it now. We all helped to paddle, as the Malays wished to put us ashore quickly and get away. As we neared land it seemed to me to be one of the loveliest looking beaches I had ever set eyes on, the sand so bright and yellow!

Close in to shore, the water was shallow — just below knee level. The Malay fishermen hurriedly put us off, said "*Salamat*" and departed as quickly as they could.

Bangka Island as I remember it

7
Kobe

AS WE WALKED UP THE BEAUTIFUL yellow sand to a higher spot on the beach, we were immediately covered with hundreds of flies. Part of their body was also bright yellow just like the sand. I remember thinking, 'How strange. Such a beautiful beach and yet all these flies.'

Of all of us, Mum and Grace were the most badly burned. They had such tender skin. We tried to get scraps of clean cloth to cover their burns as best we could to stop the flies attacking their sores.

When we started looking around the beach, we found that there were various other little groups there, English, Scottish, Australian, Americans — mostly men in uniform — survivors of shipwrecks. The *Empress of Asia* was mentioned more than once. This vessel was sunk while trying to get reinforcements to Singapore. We learnt that Singapore had fallen. I think the Dutchman in the lifeboat had mentioned that earlier as well.

We made our way inland. The town of Kobe was still under the administration of the Dutch with an Indonesian headman. Arrangements were made for our group of seven to be given a little house to ourselves.

It was a pretty little town. Unlike the *kampongs* in Malaya, here all the native houses had proper tiled roofs, not thatched and, though the houses themselves were small, they were properly constructed. The timber beams were not rough-hewn, but well formed and straight. Inside, the floors were just sand but well swept and clean.

The house we were given turned out to have a single main room in the front, with, as far as I can remember, the kitchen and a small room at the rear. We had to sleep in hessian sacks on the floor. Also, I think, we did try to put down some woven sacks or something between us and the bare sand. Sleeping two to a sack was a little uncomfortable, but it kept out the cold.

The latrine, a little way outside, was a small square wooden construction with a tin receptacle at the bottom. This was the first of a number of occasions when defecation was a problem to me. I found the arrangements so revolting that I did not relieve myself for two or three days.

After we recovered some of our strength, we went for a walk and found a place where there was a stream. It was beautiful, my idea of the perfect stream. It was approximately two-and-a-half to three-and-a-half feet deep and ten feet across. The water was clear. There was clean white sand at the bottom together with some large boulders and rocks.

I know I went in for a swim and I think some of the others did too, including Marc, June and some of the ladies.

Most of the military men had been ordered to the capital, Pangkalpinang, where they found that the Japanese were now in control and where they were detained and sent to the prisoner-of-war camp at Muntok in the northwest of Bangka Island.

Nor did our own freedom last long. One day, orders came from the capital that we had to go there too. We were directed into buses, which soon moved off along the winding road. The terrain was mountainous, and the Malay bus driver drove like a man possessed.

At the bottom of every peak was a little stream, usually bridged by four thick broad planks. He would put his foot down on the accelerator on the downward run and aim straight for the planks while we had our hearts in our mouths hoping he would not miss. He did this even from heights where we could barely see the narrow structures at the bottom. He had to do it, he declared, to gather speed to go up the other side.

Behind him, on the front seat, sat another Malay smoking a cigarette made from tobacco rolled in a palm leaf called *kretek*, which had quite a pleasant aroma.

8

Pangkalpinang

WHEN WE ARRIVED AT Pangkalpinang we were fairly well treated, and our group of seven was taken to the *Centraal* — the General Hospital. Principally, this consisted of single-storey blocks containing wards of two or four beds. External walkways linked the buildings.

Mum and Grace were still suffering from their extreme sunburn. Mum's was the worst. The blazing sun had flayed the tender skin from all over her body. Now she and Grace had their raw, weeping flesh regularly dressed and wrapped with fresh, clean bandages. The care and attention they received in that place was really like a blessing from God. The Lord must have directed the Angels to look after them. If they had not received this care and attention they would have been in a very bad way.

Dixie was not so badly burned, neither was the White Russian lady nor June and Marc. I seemed to have escaped with only slight sunburn. The other shipwrecked people who were in the lifeboats did not, as far as I know, get any hospital treatment at all before going into internment.

Our family group was allowed to stay at the hospital for some weeks, until Mum's burns had completely healed. During the early part of our stay, after we had our meals, the ward attendant used to ask '*Kenjang*?' meaning 'Have you had enough?' and offer second helpings.

The orderlies had a strange way of addressing me as *Senor*, like the Spanish, different to Singapore where boys would be addressed as *Baba*, young girls as *Missi*, the men *Tuan* and the ladies *Mem*.

The bulk of the food served was tapioca, which was like potato, only fluffier when cooked the way they did it. Eating three or four chunks of tapioca with salt was like having three or four potatoes. The second helping was a couple more chunks of the same. But towards the end of our stay they stopped offering second helpings. What was on your plate was all you got. Even boiled tapioca was becoming scarce. We heard terrible stories of what was going on outside in the town — people having their fingers hacked off to get at their rings and many other atrocities.

I was still young enough to play games and the girl, June Bourhill, always wanted to play some game or other, but I soon tired of them. We were in a slightly different age group, I was thirteen and she only eight or nine. Mum said, "She always wants to play games with you but you never want to." Marc might have been willing to play with her but — at under four —the age difference made the choice of games they could both enjoy very limited.

One thing that struck me about this place was the intensity of the storms — how the thunder would echo and reverberate through the hills and surrounding buildings. Maybe this was because the hills contained tin.

After a few weeks at the hospital the message came that we were to be transferred to Muntok, where there were other prisoners-of-war. Muntok is the town on the north west of the island where those in the lifeboats landed. As mentioned earlier, it was on Radji beach, near Muntok, that a group of men, and twenty-two of the Australian nurses from our ship, the *Vyner Brooke,* were driven down to the sea and machinegunned.

First the eighteen men were taken down to the beach behind a bluff, by a group of ten Japanese soldiers and one Japanese officer. The women heard muffled gunfire. The Japanese returned wiping their bayonets. Then the nurses and one other elderly woman were ordered into the sea. They waded into the surf until they were nearly up to their waists, then the Japanese fired on them from the rear.

Of this group of the Australian Army Nurses, only Sister Bullwinkel escaped death. She was struck by a bullet above the left hip and flung into the waves and there she floated, bleeding, among the corpses of her murdered companions, her mind screaming at her that she had to feign death or else the Japanese would finish her off with their bayonets.

So there she bobbed on the incoming tide, trying to breathe, her head half under water, and time dragged by very slowly.

Finally, she plucked up courage to raise her head a little and she saw that the Japanese had gone. The beach was deserted. She crawled up the sand and found a pathway into the jungle. A little way in she could go no further, and sprawled in the brush, unconscious.

She recovered to find it was morning and there were Japanese soldiers on the beach again. She was terrified that they would find her, but mercifully they soon marched away. She was hot and very thirsty and went in search of a spring, and found a badly wounded British soldier, Private Pat Kingsley, as well.

He was a survivor of the first part of the Radji beach massacre and Vivian Bullwinkel remained with him and tended his wounds in the jungle for the next twelve days, only venturing out at night to beg food from local natives.

They finally concluded that they could no longer continue like this, but would have to surrender to the Japanese all over again — and face what?

It took all of their courage, but on February 28th this is just what they did, and lived. But in Pat Kingsley's case not for long. Sister Bullwinkel was reunited with the thirty-one nurses who had survived the sinking of the *Vyner Brooke*, but Pat Kingsley died of his wounds shortly after.

Eric Germann was another survivor of the massacre, as was a young navy stoker, Eric Lloyd, who escaped by holding his breath and swimming under water.

After the Japanese soldiers had left the beach, these survivors made their escape. Later they met up with other shipwrecked people and when the group finally decided, a day or two later, to go to Muntok town to give themselves up they came upon this same squad of Japanese going the other way, who took absolutely no notice of them. Just walked past.

A little known ending to this horror is described by another survivor, who said a group of Australian soldiers were rounded up by the Japanese and ordered to carry the bodies of the massacred men and nurses from the beach to be burned. They had to collect all the wood and debris that they could find, build a large funeral pyre and then place all the bodies one by one on this pyre until only ashes remained.

So like Sir Edward (Weary) Dunlop who requested that, after his death, his ashes be scattered over the jungles of the Death Railway in Thailand, the ashes of these other victims of Japanese *Bushido* will remain on the site of the massacre, the Radji beach of Bangka Island.

9
Muntok

OUR DAY CAME TO LEAVE the hospital. Until now, in spite of all we had gone through, it had seemed like an adventure, in a way. When I mentioned this thought I was shouted down by everyone. "What adventure? We were nearly killed! And look at the state of us, half dead already and you call it an adventure?" I decided to keep my thoughts to myself for the time being.

We left the hospital and were driven in a lorry up the east coast of the island and then across the top to Muntok. On the way there were hills and gullies, but nothing as steep as we had encountered between Kobe and Pangkalpinang. The land was quite frequently cultivated in some form of plantation. Much of it was pepper. Stout wooden posts driven into the ground supported the pepper bushes. The stakes seemed to be in the centre of the plants which grew to about five feet high and about one foot in diameter. They stood in neat rows.

The peasants going quietly about their business, the hills, gullies and forests looking so serene, it was hard to imagine that this place was endemic with deadly diseases including cerebral malaria and beri beri that we had been warned of by the doctors before we left the hospital. Remember they said, to boil all water, even if it looks clean, and boil vegetables for at least twenty minutes.

We arrived at Muntok.

The prisoners were allocated to either the Cinema, the Jail, or the coolie lines building originally erected for the tin labourers, which was known as the 'Tin Winning Building'. The place we were taken to was too big to have been the Cinema. It had two large wings on opposite sides of a courtyard: one side for the interned civilian men and the military prisoners and the other side for all the women.

At the top, near the entrance, was a building at right angles to the two wings which housed the Japanese guards.

This must have been the 'Tin Winning Building.'

We were directed to the women's section which comprised long stone dormitories. Each dormitory had concrete slabs along the two sides which sloped slightly to the centre walkway. These were to be our beds.

All we received here for dinner was a small cup of watery rice porridge — and that was it. It was horrible. Then we had to bed down on the cold concrete slabs. At night the guards would come through from time to time shining their torches on us.

In the morning we all had to assemble to listen to a speech by the Japanese commander. He stood in front and addressed us with words to the effect that we were lucky to be alive thanks to the benevolence of the great Japanese Emperor.

"If you think you have been badly treated," he said, "you should see how the Japanese prisoners in Colombo have been treated by the British. If I tell you, you won't believe it." He then rambled on about how great the Japanese were, etc., etc.

There was one young high-ranking Japanese officer on a horse, who thought no end of himself. He had a little riding whip and used to flick it occasionally into the face of anyone who annoyed him.

In this place, we seemed to be in the midst of the tin bearing hills. When there was a thunderstorm, the thunder echoed and reverberated back and forth — boom, boom boom, and then back again, even louder than it had seemed at the hospital. June said, "Do you hear that? How different it sounds." I replied, "Yes, it is different. One clap of thunder seems to repeat itself many times." "Yes, and the ground vibrates too."

June's finger, injured on the raft, had now healed nicely.

Thank goodness we were not here for more than a few days. I felt sick already, living only on rice porridge. We were given hints that we were to be moved and not long afterwards the orders arrived. We were going to Palembang.

Mum said, "Thank God for that! Anything to get out of this ghastly place."

Muntok had a harbour of sorts, but because the water in it

was shallow there was a long pier jutting four hundred metres out into the deeper part of the sea. We were told to gather our belongings and assemble to walk from the jail to the ship. In a loosely formed column two or three abreast, with some of the younger children being carried by their mothers, the bedraggled column headed out from the jail, through the town, to the pier. And thence along the pier to the waiting boat, a small ocean going vessel.

What I do remember very clearly was how the Japanese sailors were dressed that day. I was astonished to see that they were virtually naked, wearing only 'G Strings' as they worked. It seemed nakedness did not bother the Japanese. We were led to believe that families — mother, father, sons and daughters — all bathed naked together in Japan.

Many sailors were built like sumo wrestlers. The officers, who were not much better dressed, maintained discipline by shouting and slapping the men A sailor had to stand to attention while the officer shouted 'Kurrah' and 'Baguero' and slapped his face left right and centre. They did this with the prisoners as well. Even the women. If they felt slighted while making a speech, for instance, they would send the guards into the crowd to bash the prisoners with their rifle butts, truncheons or their fists. People fell down, women shrieked and screamed. This was Japanese *Bushido* — the way of the warrior.

On such occasions, we were left to help the injured back to the dormitories, some of them so badly hurt they had to be carried back.

10

Palembang

THE VOYAGE FROM MUNTOK would take us up the Moesi River to Palembang, and then to our new internment camp. We received one bun each to sustain us for the entire journey. The ship weighed anchor and proceeded across the same strait where we had been shipwrecked. It reached the entrance to the Moesi River and made its way upstream. The Moesi River was broad but it had to be navigated carefully because of the mudbanks. The scenery was interesting. We passed the big oil refineries at Pladjoe and Sungei Gurong. Shell on one side and Mobil or Standard Vacuum on the other.

My sister Dixie asked, "What are they?" A Dutch lady standing nearby said, "They are the Shell and Esso oil refineries. And do you know," she went on, "that Shell had its beginnings around here? The person who started it, an Englishman, Marcus Samuel (later Lord Bearsted), was a collector of sea shells and that is how it got its name." We were all surprised.

After disembarking at Palembang wharf, we had to assemble, be counted, and then carry our belongings through the town. On this move we had to travel quite a distance but I am not sure whether we covered any part of it by lorry. As far as I can recall the townspeople who lined the streets did not jeer at us.

Somehow or other we eventually got to the women's camp known as Irenelaan. As it turned out this was the best place we had been in so far. It comprised fourteen medium sized brick houses, along an 'L' shaped junction of two streets which had been fenced off with barbed wire. We were divided up, about forty to each house, in which we had to split ourselves up. If there was a garage to the house, the arrangement was that it accommodated ten women. As there were seven of us, we were given a small room behind a kitchen. Those with families of ten or more were allotted a larger room.

The place we had been given was something like our *amah's* room in Singapore, but we did not grumble. In fact we were happy! After the wretchedness of Muntok this was wonderful. The person I called the White Russian lady was near the door, then came June Bourhill, then Mum, Dix, Grace and Marc. I was at the far end near the wall. We could all see out from our places.

The corner house which we were in, House 11, also accommodated Mrs Day; Mrs Simmonds; Mrs Biddell; Robbie Patterson and his mother; the Boswells, Mrs Boswell senior, her daughters-in-law and children: Charlotte, Clare, Drena, Kenny, Joan and Maisie. Kenny was about the same age as myself. He had quite a good singing voice, and could yodel. Also in the house were Phyllis Ann and Mrs Chan and her son Johnny. Mrs Chan was an English woman who had married a Chinese.

The Reids were in the house below us, House 15. Molly Ishmail and her mother, Mrs Gardiner; Olive Bayliss; Mrs Reid and her children James, Erica, Jane, Roy and Dirk.

Mrs Brown (wife of the Chief Choirmaster of St Andrews Cathedral, Singapore) was in the garage of House 9 across the road on the higher side, together with her daughter Shelagh, a young lady in her twenties. Amongst others there was Mrs Colley; Mrs Weir and a little boy called Misha; and Margaret Dryburgh.

Margaret Dryburgh was a Presbyterian missionary, a gifted artist and musician. Many of the sketches of the camp houses and, later, the camp huts were drawn by her. She rewrote almost thirty orchestral compositions for the camp choir from memory, as well as the Song of Survival. Unfortunately she was one of those who did not survive until the end of the war. Sadly, she died on 21st April 1945.

The Colijn girls, Helen, Alette and Antoinette, together with Mrs Muller and Mrs van den Haut among others were in House 16 on the higher ground.

In two houses across the road were Australian nurses who had somehow or other made it to the shore, Jessie Blanch, Jennie Greer, Florence Trotter, Joyce Tweddell,

Beryl Woodbridge, Veronica Clancy, Sister Mavis Hannah, Elizabeth Simons, Sylvia Muir and Sister Nesta James.

The civilians included the Close family: Mrs Close, Sheila, Jane and David; Mrs Tunbridge; Mrs Blake and Dennis; Miss Murray and Mrs Gilmour.

British nurses included Sisters McCullum, Rossie and Castle. Some of these nurses had been in the water for up to sixteen hours before making it to the shore at Bangka Island.

In House 9 were Mrs Tekelenburg and her daughters Katje and Elsie; my friend Hans Schoenberger and his mother and also Peter and Benny. Ade de Konig was in a house nearby with his family.

I think the Dutch Religious Sisters were in House 18, including Reverend Mother Laurentia, who was the official spokesperson for the Dutch women internees.

By the way they cared for others the Reverend Mother Laurentia and Shelagh Brown were a wonderful source of strength to us all.

We had an electric cooker in the house, which the families used in turn. On this we tried to make rice biscuits (because there was no flour), but they were not a great success.

One of the houses on the upper side across the road had a sort of verandah or patio with a low wall in front of it where the occupants had placed glasses which were filled with what looked like orange or raspberry drinks. Such luxury! We used to wonder where they got them.

We thought that they were lucky or rich, until we found out that they were just coloured glasses filled with plain water.

From the kitchen sink next to our room the water ran out to a small open drain on the edge of the garden and then down the slope to a bigger drain on the side of the road. I noticed that on both sides of the drain, where the dirty sink and soapy water was flowing, the plants and grass were lush and luxurious.

Now that we had settled into our accommodation in Irenelaan, there was time to hear the stories of how people had come ashore from the *Vyner Brooke* and other sunken ships or survived their ordeal at sea, and to remember those who had been in the water, but not been seen since.

I recall the experience of Mrs Phyllis Tunbridge who had a most intriguing introduction to the Japanese. She had worked in General Staff Intelligence at Army Headquarters, Fort Canning, Singapore. When the call for evacuation for civilian women and children came she joined a group of British Nursing Sisters, a large contingent of Australian Nursing Sisters and also a small number of servicemen's wives who had forgone the opportunity of earlier evacuation out of a sense of duty to husbands still desperately trying to turn the tide of battle against the Japanese.

They were among those evacuated on the *Vyner Brooke* and when, bombed and blasted, it started sinking, she jumped overboard and swam away from the ship's side towards the nearest life raft which, as soon as she reached it, she could see was crowded already. Indeed there were also many survivors in the water around it, clinging desperately to the cleated ropes along its side.

After a quick appreciation of their predicament, it was agreed that those who were able should swim and tow the raft to the shore, which could be seen in the distance. And this they set out to do.

They held on to the raft's ropes and swam with the other arm. But, after a while and considerable effort, Phyllis realized that they were fighting a losing battle with the strong currents running in the Strait, and were not making any progress toward land. A decision had to be made quickly while they still had some residual energy if they were to improve all of their chances of survival.

Phyllis was a good swimmer and decided that this was the moment to summon her courage and put her skill to the test. She was a very determined person and this was not the first occasion she'd had to overcome adversity in her life. Her time had now come and she called out, "Will anybody come with me to swim ashore to get help?" A response came from Sister Nesta James, an Australian Nursing Sister, and both women immediately struck out for the shore, comforted by the wishes

61

of good luck from their comrades who would remain at the mercy of the sea unless help arrived.

Daylight was now quickly fading and only small flickering lights ashore and the light from a lighthouse provided any sense of direction. It was almost impossible to gauge distance or progress as they steadily eased themselves toward the shore, swimming as best they could across the strong current and ebbing tide.

Suddenly in the early hours of the morning, after fighting their way through the breaking waves, they felt sand beneath them. They were too exhausted to stand and could only manage to crawl up the beach. They had been in the water for twelve hours since they had jumped overboard from the ship which now lay at the bottom of the Bangka Strait.

Phyllis had kicked off her slacks in the water which left her in her underwear and shirt, whilst Nesta had managed to keep her nursing sister's uniform on, but was also bare foot. After a short rest they detected the outline of a hut nearby and with a little apprehension decided to approach it. As they neared the hut a dog began to make its presence known, half-barking and half-growling. A smart retreat appeared to be indicated and they quickly made as much distance between the dog and themselves as their exhaustion would allow.

Now the only remaining hope for them appeared to be the lighthouse. It was difficult to judge how far it was in the distance but their thoughts returned to the perilous situation of those they had left behind on the raft. There was no time to rest and they must strike out for the lighthouse without delay. As it turned out it was closer than they had estimated.

They cautiously entered the open door and were greeted by a Malay family who were already awake and appeared extremely anxious. Phyllis took a keen interest in the fire burning in the corner of the room. She immediately took the opportunity to dry the several hundred Singapore Straits dollars she was carrying with her because she saw little use for them caked together and soaked with seawater, which could soon become a soggy mass of no value at all.

She took out the money and proceeded to lay it out in front

of the fire. Hopefully this would indicate to the Malays that they had the capacity to pay for goods or assistance. Although the Malays appeared friendly, they were at the same time obviously very frightened and the reason for this manifested itself only a few minutes after their arrival, when a Japanese patrol with rifles and fixed bayonets entered the room.

This was their first meeting with the Japanese and one they would not forget in a hurry. The Japanese considered it absolutely essential to unambiguously determine the gender of their captives by feeling their genital areas much to the chagrin and embarrassment of the two women.

The officer who was in charge spoke some English but unfortunately the tongues of both Phyllis and Nesta were so swollen from their ordeal that any words they tried to utter were unintelligible. They did point to their tongues and the officer responded by giving each of them a half ration pack of biscuit which was so hard that they could not even bite into it in their condition. The patrol moved on after this brief exchange, leaving three soldiers behind to guard them.

At this point things were still tense. The Malays were obviously terrified, and Phyllis and Nesta were also uneasy. They had heard of the many Japanese atrocities and their fears were not allayed when the guards made plain their sleeping arrangements: one lay down between the two women whilst the others lay down one on each side. The two women were so tired after their twelve-hour ordeal in the water that they immediately started to doze. There was no attempt by any of the three Japanese soldiers to even touch either of the women. It was still early morning when the two women fell deeply asleep from exhaustion and the guards also fell asleep.

Nobody paid any attention to the money.

In the morning the guards hurriedly left. Whether they had another predetermined assignment, or had responded to some signal, no one knew.

The Malay keepers of the lighthouse and their families were obviously tremendously relieved. They produced some coffee that tasted more like dregs than a freshly brewed pot, and asked Phyllis to return the pyjama trousers they had lent her for the night — offering in exchange a piece of cloth which she was able to wrap around herself like a sarong-style skirt. They then said *'Pigy jalan lakas'* which translated to 'Go quickly.'

Appreciating that another Japanese patrol might not treat them as casually as the first one they had encountered, they did not waste a moment and hurried back along the beach in search of other survivors.

In her haste Phyllis had forgotten her money. All their worldly goods were now represented by what they stood up in.

It was not long before they came across others from the raft who had managed to reach shore and exchanged stories. Apart from the urgent medical attention required for rope burns to hands and shrapnel wounds, they were all tired, thirsty and hungry. Their only hope appeared to be to surrender to the Japanese.

As groups gathered together on the beach they were escorted by Japanese soldiers to the Customs Shed in Muntok near the wharf. Two days later the transport trucks arrived and their three and a half years of internment as 'guests of the Emperor' started. Mercifully, they were not brutally ill-treated.

It seems that Sumatra had been placed under the Administration of the Japanese 7th Army in Singapore, and the more humane treatment afforded to us could be attributed to that fact.

I do not know whether the surrender terms negotiated by General Percival had anything to do with it but, from what I gathered after the war had ended, it appears that those who were captured and interned in Java under a different Military Command were treated much more harshly and brutally. To my mind, what also helped us was the fact that Captain Miachi, who was in charge of us, had lived in Singapore for some years before the war.

The Japanese Military Police, the *Kempetai*, were brutally similar to the Gestapo and a different kettle of fish. No administration could control them. When they got involved in anything they went about their business in a merciless and cruel manner. For example, butchering some of the Charitas doctors for allowing letters between the men's and women's camps to pass through the Palembang hospital.

In this Internment Camp there were, I believe, about four to five hundred women and children of various nationalities — Australian, British, Dutch, American, Eurasians and others. There were even Ambonese interned here due to their fierce loyalty to the Dutch. The predominant nationalities were English, Dutch and Australian.

A committee was formed, to which each household elected a person, known as the house captain, who was answerable to the authorities. The Dutch had lived here before internment, so had most of their possessions with them, whereas the British and Australians were all survivors of shipwrecks and had lost nearly everything. But the Dutch were very generous to us.

In this environment we children made quite a few friends. I remember boys and girls of around my own age — Ade de Konig (pronounced Ahday), and his sister. Theo, James Reid, Kenny Boswell, Dirk Reid, Katje Tekelenburg, Hans Schoenberger (one of my best friends), June Bourhill, Derek Woodford, Maisie and June Boswell. The Colijn girls were slightly older.

The younger children, like Marc, also had their own circle of companions. Everyone found many others to play with. I began to feel my old self, finding humour and interest in things, being able to see the funny side of the many weird situations.

My Mother said, "Please keep your spirits up no matter what happens to me." I said, "I don't think they will do anything to you. They can't murder a person of Austrian origin can they? The Germans are their allies."

She said, "I have elected to remain British, the same as your father."

Even imprisoned as we were, nothing stops the children playing games amongst themselves. Occasionally I was called 'the Professor.' Someone would wander in and ask 'Where is the Professor?' 'Who, me?' I did not think I was any more learned than anyone else. Strangely, later in life, Marc also acquired this tag.

In some climates, it usually gets hotter and very still before a storm, and when the storm breaks it provides relief. It can be very disappointing if one waits for it and it does not break. However, here we were never disappointed.

At Palembang, there was a mountain standing blue in the distance. It was beautiful to see a storm coming over it.

I began to understand what my father had meant when he talked about a storm as a *Sumatra*. From the time you first saw it, it took just two minutes before the storm was upon you. People rushed out to get their washing in, but only managed to retrieve one or two pieces before the storm struck. The rain fell so heavily that one could hardly hear oneself speak. There was thunder and lightning and rivers of water gushing down from the roof and swamping the garden. What a deluge!

I noticed the absence of small lizards *chichaks* like those visible on the ceilings in Singapore. Instead there was a larger species called *ghekos* or *tokays*, after the sound that they made, which remained hidden above the ceilings.

Hans Schoenburger, one of my friends, had tamed one of these *ghekos*. He would call it down from the roof rafters by imitating its sound, and it would approach him and drink a little milk from a saucer on the ground.

We saw Japanese lorries driving around. They were marked *Dai Nippon* at the top in front of the cab. This became the source of a joke (Die Nippon! Ha-ha). The lorries were Datsun or Nissan.

The year was changed from 1942 to the Japanese year 2602. Even the clocks had to be reset to Tokyo time. We heard that Singapore had been renamed Syonan, and the English language newspaper *The Straits Times* had been renamed the *Syonan Shimbun*.

I felt deprived at not being able to see the Sunday Tarzan colour comic strip anymore. (Or any other comic strips for that matter). I used to look forward to that.

We heard that to enforce obedience in Singapore the Japs

had cut off three people's heads with their thick heavy samurai swords and stuck them on poles on the main road in front of the Cathay Building and Cinema.

Also at the corner of High Street and North Bridge Road, Singapore, in the glass fronted windows of the Aurora Department Store they tied up a European woman and displayed her naked for the passers-by to see. It seems what they did in Manila was even worse, so I will not describe it here. Apparently their main aim was to humiliate Europeans and the white race in general in the eyes of the native population — and sometimes they carried that to horrible and gruesome extremes.

Through our own camp information centres, and by checking with friends, we picked up the beginnings of Japanese numerals.

1. Ichi, 2. Ni, 3. San, 4. Shi, 5. Go, 6. Roku, 7. Shichi, 8. Hachi, 9. Ku, 10. Ju, 11. Ju Ichi, 12. Ju Ni, and so on

Memory jog ditty. 'Itchy knee, sang she!'

Living forty to a house meant that at night people had to bed down anywhere they could. As a result the bedrooms, living and dining rooms were all occupied at night, with people bedded down over every available square foot. To leave the room one had to step over other people.

One night a couple of us boys strayed down the road to where there was a large forty-foot high silk cotton tree about twenty feet beyond the barbed wire fence. We saw a shadowy ghost like figure at the bottom of the tree. We had heard the local Malay stories of *pontianaks.* These were ghosts who had the appearance of beautiful women who beckoned men towards them. If a man embraced such a one she would turn into a hideous evil cackling fiend bent on his destruction. The man had to struggle to free himself. She would laugh like a witch while he fled in a terrified and shocked state.

According to the legend, if you were able to knock a nail

into the back of the head of the *pontianak* it would end this frightful and hideous transformation, and she would revert to being a normal and beautiful woman. The problem was to get close enough to hammer the nail into the back of her head.

We stared at the figure. *Pontianaks* were supposed to frequent cotton trees. The ghostly figure moved from time to time so we debated between ourselves as to whether it really was a *pontianak*. It was already late at night and most people were sleeping. The other boy said "Well, there is only one way to find out — let us give it a shot with our catapults. If it is a *pontianak* the pellets will go right through it." So we both loaded our catapults and fired at the figure.

The result was surprising. A thunderous roar filled the air as the figure shouted *"Kurrah. K u r a a a g h."* It was a Japanese guard who had been leaning on the tree half asleep. Two astonished boys bolted for dear life. We ran into the nearest bottom house, through the house, nimbly over the sleeping bodies, out the other end, through the next house, and so on until we arrived at our own houses at the top of the hill, where we dived into our beds, hearts pounding.

The commotion that ensued as a result of our exploit continued for a while, but fortunately for us the culprits were never identified. God knows what the Japanese would have done had they caught us. They might have been a bit lenient with young boys, but then again they might not. People had been tortured and killed for less than this.

After some time had passed, the Japanese guards were needed elsewhere and they were replaced by Javanese civil police who were much more humane in their treatment of us.

It was in December 1942 that the Women's Choir first sang for the men. The men's working party had to march past the women's camp: some distance away, but still within sight and earshot. Their wives and daughters used to get up on the ledges and even on the roofs and call out, shout and wave to their men as they passed. Of all the voices, those of the Colijn girls, Helen, Antoinette and Alette stood out. Their voices were the most powerful and could be heard above the rest.

On Christmas Eve 1942, as the men approached, there

was silence. The men wondered why. Was there something wrong? Then, as they got nearer, the choir suddenly burst into song: *Oh Come All Ye faithful.* The men slowed down, amazed. The next carol was *Silent Night, Holy Night.* Many of the men were emotionally moved. The new Javanese police who were guarding the men were sympathetic and allowed them to halt for a while, but then, fearful of their Japanese superiors, they made the men move on again at their normal pace.

Our Javanese police guards were quite smartly turned out in dark olive green uniforms, and they were taller than the Malays in Sumatra. They were friendly towards us but could not show it when the Japanese were around.

We boys would slip through the fence at the back of the houses near Ade de Konig's place and wander a short distance through the woods. A few metres on we came upon a Chinese graveyard. There was one large grave in a sort of a 'U' shape made of concrete, which we used as our meeting place. We lads would sit around on this for a while, and then return to the camp when the Javanese guard's beat took him to the furthest point away from us.

We learned a smattering of Javanese, like *assu* for dog etc., but I have forgotten most of it. I do remember, however, that it was a very expressive and dramatic language and it would have been good for Shakespearean plays.

The Japanese called their conquered puppet soldiers *Hei Ho's* pronounced 'high ho' or 'hay ho'. The Koreans and Taiwanese who had enrolled in the Japanese army were quite nasty when they were on guard duty, unlike the Javanese police.

Another meeting place for us boys was on top of a tree near the fence. There was no objection from the guards and we would climb it, and sit three quarters of the way up where we talked for a while. It was here that we decided to have a war game amongst ourselves. I was the leader of one of the teams (the White Triangle) — and we carved into the tree a white triangle symbol. Our motto 'Never Surrender' was chosen by me.

The leader of the other team was James Reid.

The boys' war game was planned among ourselves to take place in the vacant scrubland behind the 'L' shaped layout of the houses, but still within the perimeters of the camp boundaries.

There was no real animosity in the game. It was just competitive, like a game of Monopoly or tennis or football. We did not think of the teams as Dutch or British. As far as my memory serves me there were British and Dutch boys in both teams. James and I were both British. I certainly did not think of my team as Dutch, because we had both Dutch and English boys in the team.

To the rear of the scrubland we had already made cubby houses where we used to go and play sometimes. This was where the teams had their headquarters.

One day James Reid and I were under a tall fruit tree. We discussed the rules of the game and how the points were to be awarded. Using handsaws, we made weapons in the shape of rifles from packing case wood. To these we attached strips of inner tube rubber, nailed to the front. The rubber could be drawn back to the trigger near the butt.

The rifle catapults were less accurate than ordinary catapults. This was all right with us, as we felt we would not do much harm with them. We planned to use clay balls about three-quarters of an inch thick as pellets, instead of stones. We started production of the baked clay balls about two weeks before the date planned for the game.

James lived with his mother and brother Dirk and sisters in the house just below ours on the slope. Some of the team were selected to bake and stack the ammunition. My team's stockpile was kept at the rear outside our place, and one day I was shocked to find a large quantity missing. It had been raided during the night. This was a setback — but we redoubled our efforts and changed the hiding place for the pellets. Other members of the team had to be called upon to help with the production of the pellets to make up for the loss. Some of the girls enrolled on both sides as nurses.

We strengthened our cubby houses in the bushland and

called them forts. James called his 'Fort William Henry' after an existing real fort somewhere in the US or Canada. I tried to find an original name for ours.

The day came for the battle. Our fort was nearer the houses, and James' was further downhill. The battle raged back and forth for a while, and our team captured quite a bit of ground. I found myself at a spot on the far right where there was a little rise from which I could survey the situation. I felt we were already winning, and became somewhat over confident.

It was at this point, while I was standing there with my hands on my hips, that a pellet came hurtling out of the sky and struck me directly in the left eye. The effect was unbelievable. The whole sky seemed to explode. I saw flashing lights everywhere, like hundreds of kaleidoscopes, and then came the intense stabbing pain. The first aid group did their best, but it did not help. The excruciating pain continued unabated.

I was taken to our room in the front corner house. My sleeping place was near the end. I could still see out of my right eye, but the pain in my left eye was so bad that most of the time I kept both eyes closed. I think Katje and some of the others came to see me. The next thing I knew, I was being transported to the Charitas Hospital in Palembang town. There were actually two Charitas hospitals, old Charitas and new Charitas.

At the time I did not know which one I had been taken to, but as the nuns had been evicted from the new Charitas, which had been taken over for the Japanese, I presumed this was the old Charitas. The frontage was impressive with broad front steps tapering up to the large entrance door which was in the centre. A charming and gracious German lady doctor, Dr Goldberg, came towards me smiling.

Her first words were '*Sprechen si Deutch*'. I said "*Nein.*" In English I explained that I could understand a little, but could not converse. I had forgotten my German.

I was assisted into the hospital. As far as I can recollect they held my eye to keep it still and gave me an injection directly into the eyeball. There was more than one doctor around so I was not sure who did it, the tall sturdy male doctor or the lady doctor. After that I was taken to a clean cast iron bed with mattress and white sheets. A very pretty, cheerful young nun of the Sisters of Charity attended. I remember thinking she was too pretty to be a nun. I am not sure what medicine I was given, but whatever it was, it certainly put me to sleep immediately. When I awoke I found that there were bandages over my eye.

On the second day, Dr Goldberg came to see how I was progressing. The nurse removed the bandage. The doctor told me to put my hand over my good eye and open the damaged one only. She said, "What can you see?" I saw dark clouds floating around and in between tiny patches of light. They put the bandages back on.

The next day Dr Goldberg came again. This time the dark clouds were smaller and the clear areas were bigger. Dr Goldberg said I was a very lucky boy. She said I would get my sight back completely — but forecast that at around the age of fifty I would need an operation. A few days after she said this I was discharged from Charitas Hospital and sent back to the internment camp.

Her prediction proved to be quite accurate because many years later, in Australia, a cataract developed in my left eye. I was fifty-four when I had to have an operation to remove the cataract which was performed by Dr Brian Lockhardt-Gibson at Princess Alexandra Hospital, Brisbane in May 1982.

Back at the camp I learnt later about the three main sources of medical treatment in Palembang at that time. Old Charitas and New Charitas hospitals and Dr Ghani's Clinic. Nobody mentioned anything about any other hospital or any official government hospital functioning at this time.

New Charitas Hospital was first opened in 1940 by Bishop Mekkelholdt for the Dutch Sisters of Charity. The Japanese took over the hospital for their own use and gave the sisters five hours to return to their former hospital Old Charitas, which had become a school, and was also being used to house the Dutch and American technicians who were still working at the Shell and Standard Oil refineries located at Pladjoe — down the Moesi river, as well as for Prisoners of War.

Old Charitas Hospital was not very far away from the new. It was on the other side of the road — within sight.

Mother Alacoque was the Superintendent and the doctors were Dr Peter Tekelenburg — a Dutch Surgeon, Dr Ziesal — an Indo-Dutch doctor, Dr Goldberg-Curth — the German lady doctor. Japanese doctors visited.

Dr Ghani's Clinic was upgraded to a hospital to treat native patients. The doctors were Dr Ghani — after the war he became a Minister in the Soekarno government, Dr Hollweg, who was taken out of the POW Jail for this purpose, and H. Harley-Clarke, a British dentist, also taken out of camp to work at the Clinic. The Internment Camp doctor was Dr West. There were other doctors in the camp as well. It was hard to keep track because sometimes doctors were transferred in and out of the camp or sent to attend at other hospitals to treat Japanese patients.

In the camp life reverted to the sub-normal. One day a Japanese lorry drove in through the gate with a few Japanese soldiers standing at the open back, throwing out small loaves of bread or buns to the children. They did seem to like children. And we could do with that bread, for by this time we were half starved.

Apart from the storms I cannot remember anything unusual about the nature of this place except the *ghekos* and snakes. There seemed to be no frog chorus at sunset — but at times there were fireflies. When the fireflies came, there were hundreds of them. One of the girls put a collection of them under her netted dress and walked around in the evening. Very pretty she looked, twinkling all the way.

I am not sure whether the Catholic nuns provided formal education to the youngsters or not. However, I do remember one occasion when I was passing water behind some bushes a rather stern faced nun saw me and pounced. "What are you doing there?" I was surprised. "I couldn't get to the toilet in time Sister, sorry." I had thought I was hidden behind the bushes.

"That is disgusting," she said. "You have committed a sin!"

Later, when I recounted this incident to a Catholic priest in the men's camp he laughed uproariously. "That's not a sin." he said. "It may be bad manners, and rude, but it is not a sin."

There were concerts organized in the camp and for Christmas 1942 and New Year's Eve we tried to cheer ourselves up. I remember a girl named Sheila who lived across the road dressing up in a hula skirt made from straw, which seemed to cheer some boys up a lot.

Birthday cards were handmade by ourselves. Marc, being the youngest in our group, was the recipient of quite a few of these. We made them while he was out playing with his friends, using any scraps of paper we could find, sometimes colouring in the pictures, sometimes making up composite pictures from cutouts.

Other prisoners also received birthday cards made up by family or friends on any available scrap of paper or light cardboard. The more artistic of the camp inmates did indeed produce some very interesting pencil sketches of camp life and its surroundings.

Marc's Birthday Card, 1943

74

On 31st March 1943, we again celebrated Marc's birthday. He was five now! Amazing to think he had survived and reached that age in spite of all the deprivations.

Less than two weeks later some haughty Japanese officers, accompanied by guards, entered the house. The soldiers came in first and stood at the door waiting for the officers to enter. They then shouted 'kiri.' We all had to bow. It was either that or get your head bashed in. All the boys were made to take down their trousers in front of everyone while the officers walked around nonchalantly inspecting their privates. One of the officers pointed at certain boys who were then separated from the others. I was one of them.

I thought, 'What the hell is going on here?'

Then the announcement came. "These boys have matured — they are now men. They will be transferred to the men's camp."

We were taken to the guardhouse without much of a chance of saying a tearful farewell to our families.

I had always been interested in things, and have an optimistic nature. A sort of cheerful chappie, I said "We will meet again after the war." My mother said "Yes, but if anything should happen to me, Ralph, promise to remain cheerful." I promised. My sister Grace said, "If anything should happen to me promise to do your best for Marc." I promised. Dixie was there too.

We were taken to the guardhouse. Our mothers and sisters were not allowed in. They were left standing on the road outside. In the afternoon we all got into lorries with boards mounted above the front cab which read *Dai Nippon.* As usual, one of us tried to make a joke of it, but nobody laughed.

It was April 15th 1943.

The lorries moved off. The shock of it all naturally distressed us and the tears came. The dreadful pain of separation from our mothers and families was heartbreaking.

Thinking back, I suppose some of us boys were at the stage where we enjoyed joking with the young girls and the girls enjoyed the attention. This may have been noticed by the

Japanese and by others. I am not saying there was any romantic attraction. There was none as such. Yet there was definitely a change.

Whereas previously boys did not even want to include girls in their games, now they welcomed their company and commented on little things, such as how funny it was when they giggled, what they looked like, the way they talked.

A little while earlier, girls had been a bore. Now they were fun to have around.

11

Men's Camp

THIS SAD AND BEDRAGGLED LOT, utterly dejected, arrived at the men's camp.

The men immediately did their best to organize us. We were each allotted a temporary guardian to take care of us, and given a sleeping space in the thatched roofed wooden barracks. I got into my place in the barracks and must have fallen asleep immediately. In the next few days we somehow or other re-orientated ourselves.

The first things I found difficult to deal with were the communal showers. Everybody had to bathe in one large room. I kept my shorts on. As I only had about two or three pairs, if one did not dry out quickly, I could not bathe the next day, as there would be only a wet pair to put on after the shower.

The man who was supposed to be my guardian said, "Why don't you go and bathe?" I explained my problem about the shorts and told him why I felt I had to wear them. I told him I felt a bit embarrassed.

He stared at me: "You should not be ashamed of being naked. It is the men with their misshapen bodies who should be embarrassed."

I thought to myself, 'I am not Charles Atlas', but anyway I made the effort to go and bathe with the others.

In the barracks one thing that was immediately evident to us boys was the amount of vermin inhabiting the thatched roofs of the huts. In the women's camp we had come from, with its clean concrete floors and tiled roofs, vermin infestation wasn't a problem. The men did keep the barracks clean but, somehow or other, the combination of the overcrowded conditions with the material of construction seemed to draw things like rats and bugs like a magnet.

As far as the boys were concerned, whenever we could we slept out in the open. When we could, we sterilized our bedding space in the huts by regularly pouring boiling water over the slats to keep the bed bugs at bay.

The men seemed a bit more resourceful than the ladies of the camp we had left. They made things like bamboo drainage pipes for the showers; pounded stone for sulphur; and tried to extract medicines from wood, leaves and plants. As there was no toothpaste, we brushed our teeth with coconut husk, and sometimes charcoal powder.

Many of the men were suffering from sores and septic ulcers. The treatment was to boil water and clean them with warm water and salt.

Rev. Father Th.G. Elling, SC

This reminded me of what my father had told me as a child. Warm water and salt was a definite cure-all for many things. Unlike some medicines, it was harmless and it worked.

The men also managed to make a salve from coconut oil, pounded rock sulphur and salicylic acid crystals. Caustic soda was made by soaking wood ashes in water for twenty-four hours, then draining off the liquid and straining it through a cloth.

Organization in the men's camp was quite good. Within a short time I was enrolled, with the other boys, into classes taught by the Dutch Christian Brothers of the order SCJ. Mathematics was at first devoted to mastering fractions and decimals and weights and measures. Geography, political and physical, and science, history and nature-study were among the other subjects. My teacher was Brother Samuel. Religious education was also provided and I soon came into contact with the main English speaking priest of the Dutch order of SCJ. The dynamic and energetic Father Elling. This cheerful priest was a source of inspiration for all the British and American prisoners.

I said that I had been baptized already, but nevertheless they gave me a provisional baptism just in case. After that I was immediately enrolled in the Catechism classes in preparation for my first Holy Communion.

As the Dutch teachers could teach the other subjects, but not English, we were told to read a lot. There were facilities for reading because books and old and battered copies of the *Reader's Digest* were passed around. In fact, by bartering with a Chinese trader the men's camp library had accumulated over a thousand books. Things like *The Four Just Men*, Zane Grey westerns, and books about highwaymen continued to be my early favourites, also Agatha Christie's Hercule Poirot detective novels. Writing was done on any available scrap of paper, even on the back of old cigarette packets. My reading teacher advised me to just keep reading my way through a book to get the gist of it, and not break off too frequently to look at dictionaries. This was good advice.

I was also taught a bit of architectural perspective and drawing by an architect, and woodwork by a man who had a good knowledge of carpentry and joinery. I suppose they tried to keep us busy to take our minds off the horrible and heartrending sudden separation from our loved ones.

Wooden sandals, called *trompaks* were made from any available scrap of wood. Packing cases or firewood were hacked into shape with *parangs* the big, heavy Malay knives. Straps were improvised from any old material lying around, usually canvas or rubber from old tyre inner tubes. We did have some nails.

Quite a few people in the men's camp were related to people in the women's camp. For example I found the Boswell brothers there. Elder Boswell and his brother Norman, were married to two sisters Clair and Charlotte who had been living across the courtyard from us at the Irenelaan camp with their mother and their brother Kenny, who was in my age group and who I knew quite well.

Mr Colijn, the father of the three lively Colijn girls in the women's camp was also there. The Dutch had been rounded up locally. I learned that his father (the Colijn girls' grandfather) had been Prime Minister of Holland at one time. This came as a surprise to me because all I knew was that their father, Mr Colijn himself, had been Manager of Shell at Tarakan, Borneo.

Another thing that impressed me was the fact that Dr Hollweg, who worked in Dr Ghani's Clinic in Palembang, was in fact the nephew of Theobald van Bethmann-Hollweg — German Chancellor of World War I.

Something sticks in my mind about boys being enrolled into a Boy Scout type group called the 'Great Bear'. We had oblong cloth black badges with yellow stars stitched or woven. The Great Bear was chosen as our emblem instead of the Southern Cross, because that was the constellation of stars most clearly visible in thàt place.

On 30th May 1943 I had my first Holy Communion. In commemoration of the occasion the Christian Brothers made up a Prayer Book for me.

A Treasured Possession
Pages from the Prayer Book the Christian Brothers
made for me to commemorate my first Holy Communion

They meticulously wrote out the prayers in longhand, small but neat and clear. The binding of the little book was properly sewn as they had been taught, quite firm and, although small, extremely well done. The cover was made from the trouser cloth of a man's British Army khaki uniform. I treasure this little handmade book to this day.

Roman Catholic teaching was much deeper than the Anglican doctrine taught at St Andrews School. The services at St Andrews Cathedral were less formal and rigid although the format followed a similar pattern to the Mass. The moral teaching of the Anglicans was rather less positive and authoritarian and they aimed to make us all-round 'good chaps' with sports and hobbies thrown in as well as moral precepts. They also tried to teach us basic social graces, such as table manners, how to use cutlery and how to behave at junior dances.

The Catholic teaching jumped straight into the moral issues of right and wrong. Sin or no sin. There are lots of religions in the world, and admittedly they are all trying to do good. However there are aspects wherein they differ and virtually contradict each other. My view remains that if there are two different beliefs about the same thing both of them cannot be right.

The Catholics were definitely right, as God sent his own Son down from heaven to guide them. There has been an unbroken line of Popes from St. Peter to the present day, and the Cardinals, Bishops and Priests are the successors of the Apostles consecrated by the laying of hands from one generation to the next. Jesus had promised to be with them to the end of the world. Many would try to destroy his church but the Lord had promised 'The Gates of Hell shall not prevail against you.'

Roman Catholicism was comfortable, easy to follow and reassuring. Every subject was covered, straight black and white down the middle. Every issue had an answer. At last there was some certainty in things. Reassurance was given about my family, 'Don't worry, when the war is over, you will all be back together again.' We were all very sure that the

Allies would win. Sometimes a friendly Japanese guard would talk to the men and say, "You are losing battles everywhere. I don't know why you think you will win." But we were certain we would.

One day I mentioned to Brother Samuel that Father Elling was one of the successors of the Apostles. He said, "He is not a successor to the apostles because only Bishops or Cardinals can be successors of the apostles." He was right, but the whole matter blew up into a big argument and the Bishop had to tell everyone to shut up.

Regarding the religious teaching, I had my doubts on some things. 'What if I am not brave enough or strong enough to do the right thing when everyone else is doing the wrong one? What if I can't live up to what Jesus wants of me?'

My tutor's answer was: "Before Jesus came crimes were judged only on what happened. Motive and intent were not taken into account. So some people were harshly treated, even though they had meant no harm. Jesus has shown us a better way. All you have to do is your best. God does not test you beyond your inner strength. You must not have a bad intent or evil aim."

In another discussion with my tutor I asked, "What about the misdeeds of some clerics in the past?" He answered, "Priests, Brothers and other members of religious orders are human too, and as such they are subject to the same human frailties as the rest of us. The Church is at its most noble when under adversity, but unfortunately, at its most corrupt when it has absolute power. The important thing is, that in spite of all its frailties, it should never teach wrong.

"People try to justify themselves when they do wrong, and that is where the danger lies. Down all the years we have striven never to teach wrong.

"Also, keeping the Faith means doing what is right regardless of where you are, or who you are with. The test is what would you do if you thought that no one would ever find out. Would you commit a crime, or would you keep faithful to your promise, even if you are in the middle of the desert, or at the North Pole.

"If you are true to yourself and sincerely believe that what you are doing is right, nothing will shake you. Even if false accusations are made against you which others believe, do not worry. Have faith. The true facts of the matter will always come out in the end."

The teaching and guidance went on regularly for a while, but sickness and weakness were a problem.

Men died quite frequently, including teachers and guardians. When my guardian became too sick to look after me, the Christian Brothers and priests took me in with them. I found I was in a larger oblong room where all the priests and brothers had sleeping places around the walls, with the Bishop or Monsignor at the top end of the room.

There was no platform, we all lay flat on the floor. I found I was next to another English boy by the name of David.

The priests and brothers were very dedicated and spent long hours at their daily prayers, the priests more so than the brothers. The food in the camp varied with what was available at the time, and suddenly we got a daily serving of maize, which notoriously encourages flatulence. One night, after the priests had finished their prayers, we all settled down to sleep. Suddenly the deathly silence was broken by David, the boy next to me, breaking wind loudly. The next moment I, too, couldn't help myself and did the same thing. It was so funny we laughed out loud.

After this happened a few more times, the Bishop spoke up loudly from the top of the room, "Stop that!" he thundered.

One day I asked another of the priests what he thought about the native medicine men. "If these people bang their tom toms and make weird noises, stick pins in dolls and boil weird concoctions, can it have any affect on a person? Can they really put a hex on them?"

He seemed to be taken aback by the question. His eyebrows arched and his brow furrowed as he thought about it for some time, before answering. "Not if you don't believe in it."

I said, "What do you mean?"

"In the first place," he answered, "even if some power is

conjured up by whatever they do, the power of God through Our Lord Jesus Christ coming down to us through the Christian faith by the Holy Spirit is far greater than anything they can ever hope for.

"The second thing is," he continued, "do not let such matters enter your mind. It is the mind that is affected, so if you do not entertain the thought it has no effect.

"You know for yourself," he continued, "through your years in Singapore and Malaya, that these native superstitions can be just brushed aside, don't you?"

I nodded. "Ever since the scientific discoveries around the time of the Industrial Revolution in England we have known how silly these superstitions are."

"My son," he said. "Christian enlightenment came long before the industrial revolution. Our missionaries were going out to the far corners of the world long before that. At that time there were no trains, steel hulled steamships or machineguns."

I said, "Well, I know that Stamford Raffles was around these parts as well as in Singapore. He came as far down as Bencoolen and Palembang in Sumatra, and to Batavia in Java where his wife Olivia was buried. A Malay writer wrote that he and Olivia were like a king and his consort. He was energetic, talented and gifted, and amongst his other reforms took a great interest in the naming and classification of plants, establishing Singapore's Botanical Gardens. Always smiling, he and his wife were well liked by the local population."

"Yes," said my mentor, "but did you know that Napoleon's men were here earlier that that?" I was startled. I had only heard about Napoleon's exploits in Europe.

The priest went on, "They, the French, were rather harsh in their treatment of the locals, and that is why everyone couldn't wait for the British to come."

All this was news to me. I could only mumble, "Is that so." "My son," he said, "this place goes back a long way. Raffles was here between 1810 and 1815. He founded Singapore in 1819, and he died in 1826. But the Portuguese were in the

Moluccas in 1513. By 1520 Franciscan missionaries were in Timor."

I was quite surprised by this information. I turned to another subject. "What about fate?" I asked. "Fate," he answered, "can best be summed up in the words of Poirot, 'I believe in a fate that could overtake you if you do not act, but not one that overtakes you no matter how you act.' In other words, if you step out onto the road, and a bus is coming towards you, if you don't do anything you will be knocked down. If you step back, you will save yourself."

I thanked him. He said "God bless you, and remember Faith is stronger than fate."

I have sometimes found one of the commandments given by Jesus difficult to follow. 'Love your enemies.' This had also been taught to me by the Church of England teachers at St. Andrews, Singapore, but I found difficulty in loving people who tried to do me harm. I felt like having them smashed instead.

One of my friends, Theo, said "You use the word 'smashed' a lot. What do you mean? Do you want to batter or bludgeon them?" I said, "No, far from it. What I want is for them to be defeated by an overwhelming force. Imagine a giant hand holding a giant rubber hammer. This hammer has a barrel shaped head, about three feet in diameter, and five feet in size. The giant hand brings it down and slams it on the head of the person to be smashed."

He said, "It would be like a cartoon where the villain is flattened by a steamroller on the road."

Our minds wandered, "What if he gets up again. You know — in the cartoons they are flattened, yet they rise and dust themselves off and get up again."

I said, "I don't know, all I am doing is replying to your question as to what I mean by the phrase 'have them smashed.' "

Loving your enemies was explained to me by the priests. We may like a person, but at the same time not like something he does. Think of your friend taking one or your sweets or chocolates without asking. We may not dislike him, but we dislike his action. When we like a person we enjoy their company, we express our friendship, we show it by giving them gifts.

If we do not like a person's ways, because of rudeness, for example, we tend to avoid their company. They should be told so that they understand the reason for our displeasure. If they see that and try to change their ways, we may forgive them in our hearts and try to have another go because, apart from that, we did like them. If things still don't work out let them go their own way.

This is all right for strangers. But what would happen if a loved one in a family does wrong and, say, because of anger 'brother rises up and tries to kill brother' as they say in the Bible. How can we love him when he is trying to do that? We can't. But did we love him before? Yes. He is family.

The answer lies in trying to make him understand how awful his action is. Some have remorse, some don't. There is something to be said for the Eastern philosophy of the 'yin and yang' i.e. there is good and bad in all nationalities, and there is also good and bad within each one of us. It explains how good and bad co-exist side by side before circumstances thrust one to the fore.

If a thing is wrong, it has to be put right. If it is a family matter the whole family may be able to put things right. But only if they know the full story.

Secondly, people do not always feel the hurt they cause to others. Some have qualms of conscience and feel for the victim, some are callous and unfeeling. That is why the Jews had the blanket catch-all rule, an eye for an eye, and a tooth for a tooth. They sought revenge for the result, and had no thought to motive.

Jesus has taught us to forgive. So we try to reform the offender. But if the offender is unfeeling he must be punished for his crime.

There are two things involved here:- (1) Forgiveness and (2) Indulgence.

If we indulge wrongly, we are not being just, for the victim has no redress, and the wrongdoer is encouraged in his wickedness. It is a difficult situation to resolve fairly. That is why the Kings in early ages, when they were lost for an answer, would call in the priest for guidance before coming to a decision. So you had two branches of the law, for example in England there was the Common Law and when that was too harsh, people could appeal to the King, who in turn got advice from the Cardinal (who became known as the Lord Chancellor controlling Equity). Common Law could be overruled in the interests of mercy and justice.

In the Sacrament of Confession in the Catholic Church forgiveness is granted only when there is a firm purpose of amendment on the part of the penitent. The priest is bound by his vows not to divulge what he has been told. If the penitent seeking absolution cannot overcome his urge to sin again, he must keep away from the source of the temptation, known in the Church as the avoidance of the occasion of sin.

It is important to realize that there must be a solemn promise to do this. Even though religious forgiveness has been given by the priest the sin is not absolved until some penance or reparation is made.

What if someone is going to kill you? Answer: Human life is sacred. Every human being has the inherent right of self-defence. They can defend themselves by any means possible. And the animals? Answer: Man has been given complete dominance over all other living things on earth, to do as he will. (Genesis). But they too are entitled to defend themselves.

These were questions which troubled me as I grew up, and the answers I found.

Around this time, we had had to take turns to go out with the working party to do grave digging in a plot behind the rubber trees. If there was not enough room for more graves more trees were felled with axes. This part of the job was quite enjoyable as we felt we were lumberjacks. A notch had to be chopped into each side of the tree, one much lower than the other. The tree would invariably fall in the direction of the lower side notch. After the trees were felled, they also had to be cut into lengths of six or eight feet. They were then chopped into more manageable pieces.

We had also built our own trestles which we used for sawing. The saws were big and had two handles. There was one person on each side to keep the saw moving to and fro. There were two trestles, with one man and one boy, aged about fourteen, at each. One day the subject of sex came up. The men were discussing the sermon on Sunday. Even though they were half starved, one of the men said to the other he could do as the sermon directed, as he had perfect control of himself. The other man said, "You think so! What would you do if a beautiful naked woman suddenly emerged from the forest and stood in front of you here?" Another man who was doing something else within hearing distance intervened. "Not in front of the lads." he said. So they both changed the subject. We were amused, but kept silent.

The actual business of grave digging itself was a chore I disliked immensely. The soil was wet red/yellow clay. It stuck to you everywhere. It was bad enough that we had to *chungkoal* and shovel it — but it stuck fast to the implements. Instead of it flying off when you tossed it over your shoulder as expected, it remained on the shovel and came back down on you. Each spadeful had to be scraped off. Six feet down was a long way.

In the movies they go through all sorts of filthy situations and always come up fresh. In reality it was not so. After you got messed up you stayed like that. Even if you could get into the shower when you got back to camp there were few clothes to change into, and the filthy ones could not be washed and dried for the next day. In normal times, when you get a scratch, or an insect bite, you could clean it and put on salve and a dressing, but here you just had to live with it, uncomfortable or not. You had to live with all of these things. There was nothing else you could do. But you could never, ever enjoy them.

One day I became ill. I was on my allotted space in the dormitory when I started shivering violently. This went on for over an hour, then stopped. My brow was hot. After about another hour it started again. I was shaking uncontrollably. One of my friends, I think it was Hans, sat on my chest to help me stop shaking. My friends at that time were David, Hans Schoenberger, Ade de Konig, Derek, Kenny and some others. I seemed to have lost immediate contact with Dirk and James Reid. Eventually one of the camp doctors got round to visiting me — he said I had malaria. I think I got a bit of quinine.

There was not much they could do. Despite the fact that the Japanese had conquered the Dutch East Indies, the world's principal source of quinine at that time, supplies of the drug were severely limited thereafter. Lord Louis Mountbatten later claimed that malaria was a great ally of the British forces in the jungle campaigns in Burma, killing more Japanese than did Wingate's Chindits, who were all protected with new anti-malarial drugs quickly developed in the UK as quinine substitutes and generally much superior to quinine in their effect.

The type of malaria I had contracted was the 'one-day-on-and-one-day-off' type. They said it could affect you all your life. That may be so, because even though I was de-toxified after the war I still have alternative up and down days, or so it seems. It may be all in the mind.

Anyway, after a period of very severely high temperatures for about seven days, the body overcame the illness and it petered out. I noticed that some men had been reduced to skin and bone and were but shadows of their former selves. But the strange thing was, no matter how weak they had become (and some were near to death), they still kept their former personalities.

The English Oxford graduate would still talk with his affected accent — "Oh yerse, old boy, we must do something about clearing the path." The mechanic still talked and behaved like a mechanic; the politician still had the resonance in his voice; the radio announcer his clipped manner in putting his points across and the preacher his self-assured measured speech.

They felt they were what they had been before, and conditions did not diminish their personalities right up to their dying day, no matter how weak or ill they became.

After I recovered, in spite of having very little medicine, and mainly by the body overcoming the invading bacterial hordes and curing itself, I found I was taken off the grave digging work party — much to my relief.

I, of course, I didn't know what I looked like to others. I might have looked very ill and dilapidated — but ignorance is bliss.

Then there was the case of the man across the row from me, about three beds to the right on the opposite side. He was quite healthy at that time, as he had money and was able to purchase a few extra things, although I heard later that he died a rather miserable death of beri beri. While ill he kept raising both hands and clutching at an imaginary something in the air.

Before his illness, he had the habit of coming back from the communal showers then standing naked on top of his sleeping area, while powdering his privates in full view of the whole dormitory, almost as if he were giving a performance. However I found it rather a disgusting sight.

After a while one of the priests came to see him about it. He retorted in a loud voice "Why? I am not committing a sin." The priest replied, "I know you are not committing a sin but it is not very nice." After that he did it in the bath area. He was actually a flabby pinkish man.

In September 1943, while we were still in the Men's Barracks Camp, Palembang (which the men had built themselves), we were told that we were to be moved again. However, we did not know that the women and children would take our place and some of the men wrecked things before we left.

Our destination was to be that dreaded disease-ridden Muntok, endemic with beri beri and other tropical diseases. This is not to say it looked like a slum area. To all outward appearances it was a fairly neat little town — but underneath lay the roots of ill health.

Our accommodation was to be the Muntok Jail, a stone structure that before the war had housed native criminals.

We travelled in the same or similar vessels as we did

before. They were berthed on the Palembang wharfside, with the same loin-clothed half-naked barbarous-looking Japanese sailors going about their work on board. They obviously believed in only doing the basics! They did only whatever they thought practical.

The weather was hot and steamy in the upper reaches of the swampy Moesi River so the loincloth was practical. Nakedness does not bother the Japanese. Thinking back to the women's camp, in the early days at the Tin Winning Building, the Japanese guards would walk in and out of the ladies' showers without batting an eyelid. Sometimes they would pause very briefly to stare, but that was all. They never sexually interfered with the women.

When they were angry, some of them would talk through clenched teeth, with a sort of hissing sound. An animal noise.

At close proximity one could notice their behavior patterns. If interested in something that was being explained, they would say, '*Ah, so! Sodeska.*' If any problem arose, they settled the matter quickly. Their basic method was to get stuck into the crowd that was causing the annoyance, shout '*Kurrah!*' '*Baguerro.*' and bash down everyone within reach.

Baguerro meant bad.

They did the same with their own men. If a soldier tried to argue with a higher rank he was instantly slapped hard across the face. He had to stand to attention while being slapped, and shout '*Hai*', meaning yes, to whatever he was being told. If the officer was a little man and the soldier resisted, some others would come to the aid of the officer, and hit the soldier with their rifle butts till he fell to the ground. There was not much argument. It was all very basic, brutal, and quick. No charge-sheet, no CO's report and no trouble. Instant 'crime', instant punishment.

The same thing happened if you did not bow. For example, if you were lost in your own thoughts and did not notice a Japanese, you would instantly get a thundering slap, which would send your head spinning.

Taking it out on whatever annoyed them was carried to ridiculous lengths. On the boat, I laughed when one of them, faced with a mechanical device which wouldn't work, started hitting it with a baton and then kicked it over the side into the sea. Luckily, he didn't see me laughing, or I might have followed the malfunctioning machinery.

We saw the first blue outline of Bangka Island approach and then the landing with its long jetty as we got closer.

12

Muntok Goal

AT MUNTOK JETTY there was transportation this time, so we did not have to march from the pier to our quarters. The town seemed eerily quiet. No people around on the streets, only Japanese soldiers on point duty at intersections. People seemed to have their windows and doors closed.

We got to Muntok Prison. Its high walls were topped with barbed wire and its massive timber front doors were medieval in their solidity. We wondered what fate had in store for us there. It was a surprise on entering to find that everything was clean.

During the course of our imprisonment men died every day. Unfortunately these included our guardians. These were replaced but the replacements also eventually died. As a result another boy, David, and myself were quartered with the priests and Christian brothers of the Order of SCJ.

We ended up in a clean large room with concrete floor. In this room there were no raised portions — we had to put our own native woven mats on the floor. On damp days the cold of the concrete came through the thin mats. We tried putting other materials between the mats and the concrete floor, but these could not be used for long, as they attracted vermin, and had to be burned. The mats themselves attracted bed bugs, but we solved this problem by pouring boiling water over them, and drying them in the sun. Generally the concrete was cleaner than the floor of the wooden barracks.

There were about six hundred to seven hundred of us in the Jail. At first we got some fish from the boats. The new Commandant was a civilian. He was a small sized man, who did try to get some extra food for us. He was also quite nice in that he made sure there were always flowers provided for every funeral.

My biggest nightmare in this place was using the toilets. In this place everything was built in stone or concrete and the lavatories (called *jambans*) were no exception. They comprised ten oval sized holes cut in the stone, on each side of the room. The prisoners had to squat on these openings, native style, facing five other people on the other side. I don't know where the excrement went, but it must have dropped down into a hidden drain and been flushed off somewhere.

With my upbringing, I found this routine daily opening of the bowels an incredibly difficult thing to do. It was awfully embarrassing. But eventually the force of nature, which moves relentlessly on, regardless of personal feelings, caught up with me and I had to rush in there and do my business quickly. With only ten toilets for over six hundred men the situation was not funny. Toilets were occupied day and night and everyone was completely stripped of their dignity. The best we could do was to try not to look at each other.

We were in this jail from September 1943 to February 1945 — about a year and a half.

On day I was sitting on the ground near a large archway between two sets of buildings. I had developed wind in the stomach, but every time I wanted to blow it out, someone came along to walk through the archway and I was too embarrassed to do it, and held it in.

Then I began getting gripes. I was taken back to my spot in the Priest's dormitory. I quickly developed a high fever and could not swallow. All eating and drinking was difficult. One priest came to my aid, Father Elling. He sat by me and every now and then tried to get teaspoons of soup down my throat.

I had a recurring nightmare where I saw people in the dark corner of the room beckoning me to come to them. I said "No". I became semi-conscious, then slipped into the dream again, and they were there again at the far end of the dark room, beckoning me to come.

I said, "I am not coming."

Unbeknown to me, the doctors had diagnosed my illness as blackwater fever. I sank into semi-consciousness again, Father Elling was speaking, "Come on, just one teaspoon." I shook my head, but my head was tilted back, and the soup was forced into my mouth until I couldn't help but swallow.

Eventually Father Elling and some others, I don't know who, managed to get a whole cup of soup down my throat. I started looking around again. I had been semi-delirious for over seven days it seems.

When I recovered, I asked, "Where is my cat?" Father Elling said, "You've eaten it."

I was a bit taken aback, but he said, "We had to make some soup to save your life otherwise you would have died."

Although, on this occasion the jail was clean when we got there, the whole top section of Bangka Island, where Muntok town is situated, was known for its high incidence of tropical diseases, beri beri and cerebral malaria in particular. Fortunately I did not get those diseases but there were many who did.

I think we boys were given a slightly extra ration, as we were growing lads and this helped.

The minimum daily food requirement for an adult in a warm climate engaged in light duties is: 3,200 calories for men and 2,300 calories for women. I don't know what we were getting but it was so far below this that most men were down to skin and bone. Two or three died every day. The camp population dwindled. Just when we thought we were getting a bit more room, the Japanese brought in more prisoners from other places.

It made sense to cut things up into tiny pieces. For example if you got a piece of ginger say a half inch cube in size, you could make it last for a week, say, by cutting it into four portions and storing them in your closed biscuit tin (which substituted as a billy). Then each time you got a small cup of miserable tasteless soft boiled rice, you could add a few of these bits to it, and it would improve the taste remarkably.

Similarly with beans, and other things like scraps of dried salt fish — a few tiny bits taken out of the tin every day did wonders for the meal. Generally you only needed trace elements of everything to keep going — even vegetables — or so it seemed to me. Having a tiny piece of lettuce or *kang kong* (Chinese green leaf vegetable) a day was better than eating the whole leaf and having nothing the rest of the week.

During this period the Japanese did seem to scrape around for some food to give to us. On occasion we got a fair supply of Red Palm Oil. Everything fried in the oil became reddish, but we welcomed it. Also it was quite tasty.

Another time, we got a sack or two of maize (Indian corn). Even though maize is rich in Vitamin C, it is in a form that is not easily assimilated by the human body. Unfortunately our stomachs were not used to these things, and we all got the runs. Some got over it, but others did not, and their diarrhoea deteriorated into dysentery.

There was a local plant called *seri awan* which was said to be a cure for dysentery, but during that time it was not easy to acquire. The already overcrowded dysentery ward became even more overcrowded. Contact with dysentery meant without extreme care you could get it yourself — so volunteers to tend the sick were few.

Only the Catholic priests and Brothers volunteered for the job. Bishop Mekkelholt said he would let them provided they were in charge of running it. This was agreed and soon the Catholics had to help look after the beri beri ward as well. 'Greater love hath no man than that he lay down his life for a friend.'

It was here that I saw that the Catholics practised what they preached. There were about thirty brothers and priests when we first arrived, and in the next six months or so we lost nearly half of them.

As the sick were lying on concrete platforms on either side of the centre passageway in a forty foot room it was possible to hose out the run twice a day, and clean up individual patients too. The same thing was done in the beri beri ward. The patients were individually cleaned every morning, and then the platforms were hosed off so that they had a clean bed to start the day.

Many of the priests and brothers who were given the last rites were taken to what became known as 'McDougall's Bedroom and Morgue'. It was William McDougall's own sleeping area, which he frequently gave up to terminally ill patients.

97

William McDougall was one of the Americans in our camp. He had been a newspaper correspondent in Shanghai and when he came to our camp he met Father Elling and helped him with the translation of his sermons from Dutch to English. After the war he became a bishop in one of the cities in America. I think it was Salt Lake City.

As the patients' condition deteriorated, the stench got worse. The beri beri and dysentery wards had to be hosed down twice a day — sometimes more often.

Beri beri starts with a build-up of fluid in the legs, and the legs get very swollen. It was noticeable that when you pressed your finger on the swollen portion of the leg, it didn't spring back out again quickly. The dent remained for some time. Slowly the fluid builds up higher and higher in the body.

When the beri beri patients got worse they started making a sound. It is hard to describe the sound. It was somewhere between a humming sound and a moaning wail. The sound seemed to rise and fall and it went on for hours. Once one person started, the others would follow suit one by one, until they had all joined in.

Beri beri could be cured with doses of Vitamin B so this vitamin became all-important. The wealthy managed to get it somehow, and they recovered.

In natural food, bean curd was the best source of Vitamin B, followed by boiled green gram (*katchang ijau*). A small cup of green gram would fetch up to 100 guilders. The purchasers felt it would save them from Death Row and it did.

Japanese occupation money had little value as it was just printed paper and had no backing or substance. All the old Colonial currencies such as Straits dollars, Dutch guilders, francs, US dollars and so on maintained their value, however, and were prized. Gold retained and even increased its value. People who had small gold rings or other ornaments to barter became better off; they were amongst those who now had some money to spend.

One of the Indonesian Doctors — Dr Ghani was in Palembang at the time. He saw the value of gold when all else failed. After the war Dr Ghani became a Minister in the

Soekarno cabinet. I wonder whether this influenced Indonesia to rely so heavily on gold to back their country's economy.

Many years after the war ended I heard a story about something that happened in one of the Prisoner of War Camps in Burma. Prisoners were in the jungle, sleeping around a fire, with the makeshift wooden latrines some thirty feet away.

A Japanese guard sitting near the fire dozed off, with his rifle in his hands. In the knapsack on his back, there was a bottle of vitamin pills. One of the prisoners crept up and slowly plucked out the bottle, without waking him. The prisoner got back to his place safely, and took two tablets, keeping the rest.

A few minutes later, the guard woke up and realized something had been stolen from his knapsack. He shouted, 'K u r r a h!' in a thundering voice, and ran around knocking down people in his rage.

The prisoner who had stolen the vitamins panicked and did not know what to do. In desperation, and on the spur of the moment, he swallowed the contents of the whole bottle, and threw the empty bottle into the campfire in the centre. This man already had a swollen abdomen with advanced beri beri.

The Japanese could not find the culprit, and after bludgeoning down a few people with their rifle butts they dropped the matter.

Half an hour later, the man in question got up and went to the toilets to pass water. He came back, but ten minutes later, had to go again. This went on all night and eventually he decided to stay there. He was completely dehydrated and it was a wonder he did not die. In the morning he was found, looking very much thinner with his stomach shrunken and with the bones of his rib cage showing. He was exhausted but managed to drag himself up for the *Tengko*, the rollcall and headcount. He made an amazing recovery.

As Christmas 1944 approached, Father Elling himself became ill. He had malaria and dysentery and was in the sick ward with the others. Fortunately he pulled through, though he was still very weak. Father Bakker also was unwell, but he managed to stumble up and say Mass on Christmas Day.

For the first time in all those years, the Japanese decided to allow Bishops to visit the women's camp on Christmas Day to officiate at the Christmas service.

Bishop Mekkelholt went. He said later that the nuns had sung at High Mass. He said the women's camp comprised nine wooden barracks on a hill and seemed a better place than the place we were in.

The Bishop had been given some statistics. He told us, on his return, that there were six hundred and ninety-eight inmates in the women's camp, including about one hundred and fifty children. He said that in spite of everything the Women's Choir was still singing and had sung the Christmas Carols.

In our camp Captain Seki allowed the men to kill one of the pigs for Christmas so we all got a small portion, as well as some coffee as a special treat.

There was no concert that year. In past years I had been given a small metal triangle to play in the band. I was supposed to keep time with the music.

In the first week of January, we boys got some good news. We were to be allowed to go to the Women's Camp to visit our mothers. On the appointed day, the 9th of January 1945, we all headed off there. When we arrived, we stood waiting on the grass outside, for them to come out. Suddenly the gates opened and out they came. Some saw their mothers, some their aunts, and ran to them.

In my case my sister Grace came out smiling as usual. We ran to each other and hugged, crying with joy. She said Mum and Dixie could not come out because they were still in the sick ward. I asked, "How is Marc?" She answered. "He is fine, he is a big boy now."

I asked if she had received the wooden cigarette case which I had made for her. I had carved it out of a nice piece of teak and polished it at my carpentry classes in the old camp. I had entrusted it to a Javanese guard at Palembang who said he knew where my family was, and would give it to Grace.

She said she never got it. All too soon the ten minutes visiting time was up. We hugged and clung to each other as long as we could.

Then the Japanese guards separated us, and led the women back inside and the wooden gates closed.

After settling back into the daily routine at the men's camp, we heard the news that, once again, we were all going to be sent back to Sumatra.

So, towards the end of March 1945, or in early April, we headed once again for Muntok Pier. We were taken down in lorries instead of having to march all the way. It was only when we got there that we had to trudge down the length of the long pier, bundles slung over our shoulders, past the impassive guards stationed along the pier at intervals. They watched our progress without reaction. People fell, sick stretcher-cases died — but the guards did not budge an inch nor blink an eyelid. Only the few soldiers in charge took any notice of what had happened.

There followed much going back and forth and waiting, having another head count and waiting again, only to be told in the end that we definitely wouldn't be boarding that day.

There was nothing for it but to bury the dead at sea. Dumping them over the side of the pier into the ocean would be a more blunt way of putting it — although a few words were said in prayer before that. A priest or minister would be allowed to come along and speak the words. There were no flowers here.

Then it was back to the shore again.

Day 1

Eventually, in the morning, we were all told to board the ship. So we stumbled down the pier again with our belongings, and got into small boats which took us out to the ship. It then upped anchor and travelled during the daylight hours.

We got to the mouth of the Moesi River in late afternoon. The sunset was beautiful. As darkness approached the ship dropped anchor. It was not considered wise to try to navigate the Moesi River at night as it had mud flats at various places, and swamps and jungle around it.

The sick, especially those ill with dysentery, could not help themselves. It was here that the Roman Catholic priests and Brothers again came to the rescue, running or staggering up and down with bedpans and throwing mess over the side. The work was almost continuous. On this occasion I noticed others from other denominations, and even laymen who tried to help as well.

Most of this journey must have been pretty bad because my mind is a blank on some facts. I don't even remember where or how I slept.

Day 2
In the morning the ship weighed anchor and we chugged up the now familiar river once again. On reaching Palembang we got off the boat, and made our way to the Railway Station, where we waited for a train which did not pull into the station until the evening. For some unknown reason it did not leave straight away but remained stationary. So we were locked in all night.

Day 3
The train began moving early in the morning. Some of us were jammed into carriages, others into the goods wagons where there was even less air. It was stifling. We arrived at the town of Loebok Linggau towards evening. I think we were given some soft boiled rice and then locked in the carriages again. It was stifling and the air had become putrid. Details of what was happening were becoming a blur. I had reached a state where I just did not care anymore whether I lived or died, propped-up, semi-conscious between two others.

Day 4
Mercifully when morning came we were at last allowed out into the cool morning air and consciousness floated back. We were directed into lorries for the twelve-kilometer drive to Belalau.

The driver drove like a maniac — it was reminiscent of our

breakneck bus ride from Kobe to Pangkalpinang. We seemed to be getting to higher ground, and we saw that we were approaching mountains, blue in the distance.

Although I did not know it at the time, these were the Barissa Mountains, a range that runs like a rib up the west coast of Sumatra. The city of Bencoolen on the other side of the range, facing the Indian Ocean, was of interest to me as my father believed that some members of his family had once worked for the administration there, in the early days of colonial rule.

Bencoolen had belonged to the English from 1685 to 1825 but it was a few hundred kilometres away to the south from where we were at Belalau so I never actually reached it. I wondered what the beach would be like there. Sand, I thought, not swamp as we had encountered on the East Coast.

As we came to the foothills the cicada chorus rose to a crescendo in the jungle around us. I noticed large wild gutta-percha trees, the source of indiarubber. There were strange bird sounds and warbling. The temperature seemed to fall slightly and the vegetation changed. All around the forest flourished and thrived.

Suddenly I was glad that I had not died the night before.

13

Belalau - Loebock Linggau

BELALAU was actually an abandoned rubber estate and quite big in comparison to those that I had seen in Malaya. The long huts which we were to occupy had been the coolie lines of the former rubber tappers.

Everything was in a state of rack and ruin, but the concrete floor of the huts, although cracked and pot-holed in places, still held. There were the usual raised platforms on either side of a passageway for us to sleep on. In addition, there were racks running along above the platforms on which we could keep our belongings.

We went to our places and looked around. We were warned that there was hookworm in this area — so we were to keep our feet covered at all times. Around the huts, jungle undergrowth had sprung up amongst the rubber trees.

There was a cheerful stream running through the camp. Noticeable was the glistening shiny new barbed wire at the entrance, over the stream and surrounding the camp. However the huts had not been cleaned. They swarmed with all manner of vermin. We were told to shake out our clothes or give them a sharp snap — like cracking a whip — before putting them on. One boy did this and a scorpion shot out. The look of shock and amazement on his face at the sight of the scorpion sent us into fits of laughter.

At least the outlook of this place was nice, with the rubber trees all around like a forest instead of the bleak high stone walls of Muntok jail.

Along the stream were hundreds of butterflies. Their colours were exquisite. I thought 'How can such beauty exist in a place like this where people are dying daily from disease and starvation?' Some of the butterflies were as large as small birds. I would sit and watch as they fluttered between the plants and I envied them their freedom to go wherever they pleased.

My enduring hope and, I suppose, the hope of all of my companions, was that someday we would enjoy once again the freedom possessed by these beautiful creatures. And, please God, let it be soon.

Captain Seki's house was upstream from us on the left, with the soldiers' quarters towards the right. As there were others living upstream as well, the river was soon polluted. But at least it was running water and from a distance it seemed sparkling clean and clear amongst the big boulders. So the whole scene had a much more cheerful aspect.

As far as the dirty dormitories went, we boys solved the problem most of the time by sleeping outdoors, thus getting away from the bed bugs and other creepy crawlies which came out at night and we boiled all the water from the stream before drinking it.

The Japanese did not seem to care much what we did within the camp. We had to line up each morning for *tengko*, but that was all. Captain Seki tried to tell us how to pick certain edible leaves from the surrounding area, for example the tips of tapioca plants, the tops of young ferns and the bamboo shoots. We were each given a small garden plot in which to grow something extra for ourselves. This had happened before in Palembang, but at least here there was more space to do it.

I grew tapioca, ginger, long beans, green gram, French beans, maize and radish. The last two were a failure, but the ginger, tapioca and green gram came up well.

One of the Dutch doctors, Dr Kampschuur, was a marksman, and suggested to Captain Seki that he be allowed to go out into the jungle and hunt wild boar at night with a gun and a light. I think two men were allowed out once a week, with a few bullets. The pigs came out at night to feed, and the kill rate was high.

The Japanese took the best parts of the meat. Some was, I think, sent to the women's camp. Our share was divided up into tiny portions. We got three or four half-inch portions each. One week, the hunters came back with a tiger, so we all had a few cubes of tiger meat in our soup for the first time in our lives. The tiger meat scratched my throat a bit as I swallowed it.

What individuals ate on their own was up to them, but what went into the communal cooking pot was checked by the doctors as being suitable for human consumption. They passed the tiger, and had previously allowed dog and other things, but they would not allow rats to be eaten.

In this camp you could do your own cooking, provided you had something to cook, and a fireplace to cook it on. Inmates constructed their own fireplaces out of bricks or river rocks, and thus were able to boil their water on a wood fire, although sometimes it took a while to boil.

It was about this time that I noticed that one of the men had a small kerosene cooker: a little metal box oven with a hotplate burner on the top. I said to my two friends, Hank and Daniel, "Isn't he lucky?"

Daniel said, "Mr Westerhouse, in the end block has a large clay pot stove. That's got a small oven underneath as well."

Hank said, "It seems that when there's no electricity the people who've just got really basic things are better off than the rest of us."

It struck me then. "Do you realise," I said, "that if the whole world were destroyed, and only a few of us were left, we might never be able to discover how to make electricity ever again?"

"Yes," Daniel nodded. "I wonder why they didn't teach us that at school?"

"Don't worry," said Hank. "We could still get by all right with a kerosene stove."

"And what would you do for a light?"

"Use a match."

Daniel chipped in, "What if there were no shops, Hank. No matches and nowhere to buy kerosene?"

"I'd ask the natives. They can make fire without matches and they use kerosene most of the time."

Daniel retorted. "They use kerosene all right, but if there were none left would they know how to get it out of the ground?"

I said, "Turpentine comes from a tree." An argument then arose as to whether kerosene was a mineral or came from a tree. It was a mineral.

"Anyway," I said, "the fact of the matter is that we don't really know how to get anything."

"Maybe we could ask the men." Daniel said. "One of them might know."

"At least I can make a water pipe," said Hank, whose tutor was a plumber.

In the early stages there were a few fish in the stream, but they dwindled. There seemed to be some things growing beyond the wire, within fifty feet of the perimeter itself.

Barter trade through the *Hei ho* guards increased, as did the black market. Watches, fountain pens and treasured personal items were in demand, and could be exchanged for such things as tapioca, coconut or red palm oil, or chillies. It was great to get a few pieces of tapioca. When boiled with salt it became like potato — a bit fluffy on the outside as I have already reported — and quite tasty. It was so much like eating a potato that its Malay name was *Ubi Kayu*. *Ubi* means potato, and *kayu* means wood. If left in the ground too long the *ubis* became hard, like wood.

It was quite easy to grow things in that rainy area with its orange clay soil. The only difficulty was trying to determine the right time to reap our crop. In our impatience and hunger we tended to dig the tapioca plants out too soon, so instead of three-inch thick *ubis* got only thin lengths.

The strange thing was that the few extra scraps of food we now obtained and devoured only made us more hungry. Some men used to sneak out at night to get some of the *ubi*. They became known as the *Ubi* Raiders. If there was any extra, we boys usually got some.

One day three of us boys decided to try to creep out and see if we could get any for ourselves. Along the side of the stream, towards the bottom end of the camp, there was a three-foot diameter concrete pipe leading from the estate, outside the boundary, into the stream which flowed through the camp.

The *Hei ho* guard was usually at the corner, some distance away from where the storm water pipe opened into the stream. When it was dark we said, "Come on, let's go."

We all crawled through the pipe, one by one. The trip was quite successful except that when we got out at the other end, I said, "Darn, I have got a leech on me." All other boys said "Me, too. Me, too."

We could not talk too loudly for fear of attracting the guards' attention and could not get the leeches off without tearing our skin, except by means of tobacco or salt — neither of which we had with us.

Nevertheless, we were determined to get some food, so we went about twenty yards further, got whatever we could, and hurried back. We scrambled back through the storm pipe, crossed the stream, and got back to the hut, where someone gave us bits of tobacco. We squeezed the tobacco juice on to the leeches, and they dropped off.

However, some boys were not so lucky. On a few occasions I was myself detailed to take food to some poor devil who had been caught and locked in solitary confinement in darkness, in a basement cell for a month, as punishment.

On the two or three days that I had to take the food to him, I was shocked by what I saw. Eyes bulging, staring about wildly, the prisoner came out to take the tin plate when the guard unlocked the door. He must have been living in the room with his own excrement. The sight was too horrible to behold. The guard quickly pushed me away. When I told the other boys about it, we decided not to risk going out any more.

One day a game of football was arranged between a Japanese team and the camp inmates. The camp picked out its fittest players and the game was played where the rollcall was held in the mornings.

All those who could stand had to come out and watch. We lined all four sides of the pitch. I had a handkerchief round my neck, with the knot tied in front. The game started and our players seemed to hold out quite well. In the middle of the game, without warning, and seemingly for no reason, one of the Japanese players suddenly left the field and headed in my direction. He came right up to me, stopped, and then grabbed hold of the knot in my handkerchief, pulled my head down, and shook me left to right about four times. He then went back onto the field and resumed play.

I was more surprised than hurt. "Why did he do that?" I asked. I thought that it may have been because he did not like the handkerchief tied around my neck. "You laughed at him," one of the boys next to me said. "I didn't laugh at him." "Yes you did. You did it very quietly but you did laugh when he missed the ball," he said.

By this time I had already had my Confirmation, and been enrolled as an altar boy. The altar boys here had red robes. We had to assist during the Mass by handing things to the priest, carrying the missal from a stand on one side of the altar to the other, and give our responses in Latin.

After Mass we all usually prayed for somebody. At that time it was for Churchill and Queen Wilhelmina of the Netherlands, as well as President Roosevelt.

I prayed hard for an end to the war and for liberation as well.

14

The Day Dawns

ONE DAY WE WERE ALL called to assemble between the rubber trees on the grassy lawn on the hillside, not far from Seki's house. On the day before we had received increased rations. It was now past midday.

A few days previously the *Hei ho* guards had been removed. They had been replaced by a Japanese machinegun platoon. One of the boys said, "Maybe they are going to machinegun us." We were told to sit on the grass. My friend said, "This is it, they are going to finish us off." Which, I heard later, was exactly what the Japanese did to some of their prisoners on this day in North Borneo.

It was the 24th of August 1945.

A table was placed near the top of the slope, between the rubber trees. Captain Seki was there, and started talking in Japanese. We boys were a bit apprehensive, wondering what was going to happen. I was about sixteen and a half at that time, and thought, 'I hope they're not going to kill us. This would be a rotten time to die.' Then the interpreter started translating Seki's words into English. His address was in the polite form instead of the usual guttural shouting.

"The war is over," he said. "And now we can all be friends again." He droned on while we sat there, stunned. "The Americans are fighting cruelly and mercilessly with a new type of bomb. It is called the atom bomb . . ." he rambled on.

We were happy, but feared something would go wrong. To put it another way, we couldn't believe our ears. Then it slowly began to sink in. From the gist of the translation we gradually began to realize that it was real. Japan had finally been defeated.

Words cannot describe our feelings. It was as if the weight of ages had been lifted off our shoulders. The rest of the gathering must have felt the same, but was too stunned to react.

Captain Seki was still speaking. One particular sentence caught my attention. "Men and women will be free to visit each other's camps."

He went on again about how 'We could all be friends.' The boy next to me said, "Fat hope he's got."

Captain Seki continued, "I have done my best for you . . ." I said to my friend, "I suppose in his own way he has done his best. He had allowed us a couple of bullets to go hunting, and helped us to grow vegetables."

"Soon" Captain Seki said, "American and British soldiers will be coming." Eventually the speech ended, and we all trickled back to our quarters.

The first noticeable thing was an increase in the size of our rations. The quantity was more than tripled almost immediately, and the quality greatly improved too, with less food that was actually rotten. We were told by the Camp Committee that the Allies would shortly be making air drops of supplies to us and, at the same time, cautioned us not to eat too much too quickly. "It can cause death if an individual suddenly gorges on food after many years of starvation. So be prudent. You don't want to die now, after coming this far, do you?"

When we boys went near the Japanese guardroom I was amazed. The guards bowed to us instead of us having to bow to them. We bowed back, either from force of habit or just politeness, and that pleased them. They handed us their rifles.

The guards then beckoned us into the guardroom, where there were stacks of brand new jungle green uniforms, belts and boots and we checked them against each other for fit. I cannot remember exactly, but I think we each got three sets of uniforms, two sets of boots and one leather belt. With these new acquisitions our spirits lifted somewhat. We got back to our bunks arranged the guns, spare uniforms and spare boots on our racks, and put one set on in readiness for our journey to the women's camp, which was only a few miles down the road, to look for our loved ones.

The way was pointed out to us, and along with others I

trudged in the direction of the camp. When we arrived, there was a great mass of people everywhere. It looked like a flea market or a crowded bazaar. We had to push our way through and all kept asking if anyone knew where *our* families were.

We came across old friends and acquaintances. They said "You boys look good in your new green uniforms." Some nurses also said the same thing.

I couldn't wait for my mother and sisters and Marc to see me. How pleased they would be. At last I got to the right hut. There was the usual walkway down the centre and platforms on both sides with all the ladies on their bunks. Marc was pointed out to me and I went to him. He recognized me immediately and came straight to me. He was happy to see me. We gave each other a big hug. "My, how big you've grown," I said. "Where's your Grandma?" He said, "She died in Muntok."

I was shocked. My mother, *dead*?

"Where's your mum? Where's Gracie?"

"Dead." he answered.

"Dixie?"

"Dead."

My heart sank. "What! Are all of them dead?" I said. "Who is looking after you?" Marc pointed to the lady next to him. She seemed a very nice person. I turned to her and she explained that all my family had died in the last year of the war, Gracie and Dixie only a few months before, in April.

I think the lady's name was Mrs Blake. Gracie and Dixie died within a week or ten days of each other. Dixie just before we left Muntok on Bangka Island, and Gracie very soon after we got here.

The lady gathered together what little there was of the family's personal effects and bundled them up with Marc's clothes. She kissed Marc goodbye and told him to be a good boy.

We two then started the trek back to the men's camp. On the way my mind was in turmoil. My original feeling of overwhelming relief and exhilaration at the end of the war was now replaced by grief, shock and horror. My mother,

Dixie and Grace were all gone and I would never see them again.

Marc was talking at my side. "Is it far to go now? How big is your camp? Where will I sleep?"

Strange how the very young can quickly get over a terrible tragedy. My mother's words came back to me: 'If anything happens to me Ralph, cry, but don't be morose or gloomy or downhearted. Get back to being your normal cheerful self.'

I answered the boy. "Not far now. The camp's quite big and you will be able to stay with me."

It was not difficult to get space for him to be bunked down next to me. So many of the men had died that there was now plenty of room.

I thought I would do my crying in the night, when all had gone to sleep. I stared hypnotically at the wall for some time, until what I saw became a blur. Then I tried to pull myself together.

I couldn't cry here. Although it was night, and many bunks were empty, there were still people all around. I got up and went out to the toilet, and then slowly made my way down to a grassy patch beside the fast flowing stream. There I lay, and sobbed my heart out.

The Grave of My Mother
Mrs Theresia (Resie) Armstrong
at Muntok, Bangka Island, Sumatra, 1945

Photo courtesy of the Imperial War Graves Commission

The Grave of My Sister, Grace
Mrs Grace Anna Watters-Pryce
at Belalau, South Sumatra, 1945

Photo courtesy of the Imperial War Graves Commission

The Grave of My Sister, Dixie
Miss Dixie R. Armstrong
at Muntok, Bangka Island, South Sumatra, 1945

Photo courtesy of the Imperial War Graves Commission

15

Freedom

I MUST HAVE FALLEN ASLEEP, because the next thing I knew it was morning. I heard voices. The men were coming down to bathe in the stream.

I quickly got up and went back to the hut. Marc was awake. "Where have you been?" he said, "I was waiting for you." I replied, "I went down to the stream, I'll take you there, but first let's go and collect our breakfast."

For the next day or two, before the airdrops arrived, I told Marc I would try to get to the *ladang,* the small farm close by, to try to get some extra food. I got my rifle off the rack, and three of us boys ventured out in the direction we thought the *ladang* might be. The other boys brought their rifles too.

Following the path, we left the rubber trees and got to the jungle proper. The foliage became quite dense, but there was still a trail of sorts. We went on and came upon a deep gorge. There was a river or stream running at the bottom. Across the top of the chasm, from one side to the other lay the trunk of a gigantic tree. The trunk was so enormous that a rickshaw or a small car could have driven across it quite easily. How they had felled it, and got it to lie so precisely across the gorge was a source of wonderment to me. On the other side, lower down the slope, we could see the *ladang.* Also tapioca and pepper planted in neat rows with, nearby, three native houses standing on stilts. We walked across the fallen tree trunk to the other side. It was so broad that we did not feel any sense of vertigo at all, even though it was high above the chasm. Once across there was a dirt track down to the houses.

The Malays seemed to be frightened. They went indoors and kept peering at us. We told them it was all right to come out, the war was over, but they said, "Hide, hide quickly, the Japanese are coming."

We looked around, and sure enough there were two Japanese soldiers coming down the dirt track towards us.

When they got near us they let out a thunderous roar, in their usual manner, and saluted us. We acknowledged by saluting back, and they then walked on past and disappeared down the path.

The natives could not believe their eyes. They came down their ladder and expressed their joy by jumping up and down. They invited us upstairs and gave us a meal which we ate on the mats. The food was quite delicious and we relished it, as we were still half starved.

They asked us what had happened. We told them that Japan had been hit by two massive bombs that were so powerful that each of them had destroyed an entire city. After that they began bartering with us, offering half a dozen eggs in exchange for pieces of clothing. Even whole chickens. We exchanged our shirts and even our socks and our boots for food but were determined not to part with our trousers or rifles. They did not ask for the rifles anyway.

Finally we left them, arms laden with goodies, but half naked and barefoot and made our way back to the camp. Marc was pleased to see that we had brought back quite a lot to eat, including sweet potatoes, yam, tapioca, hens' eggs and one live chicken. The other boys had similar items.

We now had to decide how to kill our chickens before frying them. We decided that the most humane way would be to cut off their heads with a *parang*. So while one boy held the chicken with its head on a wooden block, another swung the *parang*. The neck was severed in one clean sweep, but the chicken then twisted out of his hands and we were astonished to see the body running off without its head.

We all ran after it, and finally caught it. Then the same process was repeated with the other boys' chickens. We plucked the feathers off my chicken by first immersing it in hot water, Marc and I then cut it into pieces, rubbed the pieces with rock salt and fried them in oil. I think it was red palm oil. It was delicious.

However, we agreed that we must not eat too much all at once, and we kept the other pieces in an empty Jacobs Cream Cracker biscuit tin in the shelf above our bunk.

After about half an hour, Marc said, "Do you think we could have another piece?" So I said, "Very well," and we had another piece each. It wasn't very long before that fried chicken disappeared completely with only the bones left, picked clean.

The next day Marc, myself and some of the other boys went down to the stream for a bath and swim. There were boulders in the stream and the water at this upper end was quite clear. All of a sudden there was a shout, "They are coming, they are coming."

We looked up and saw two large planes approaching. They had four propellers each.

A big square had earlier been marked out in the centre of the parade ground of the camp. While the planes were still on their run-in, they started dropping the cylindrical food containers. The parachutes opened and the containers floated down. They were large. Most of them dropped into the field, but one missed it and floated out into the rubber trees.

We dressed hurriedly and ran in the direction of the stray container. There were already some people there trying to drag it back to the camp. It was left to the Camp Committee to share out the contents and this they did fairly. The small containers holding K-rations, food and other things were distributed to each and every one without delay — but again with the warning that we were not to eat too much at one sitting.

The Allied forces who had parachuted down to take over from the Japanese were stationed in the town of Loebock Linggau about seventeen kilometres away. Three or four boys, myself included, decided to walk there to see them. It was to be a morning excursion. We put on our green uniforms and boots and headed off. We did not take our rifles with us. If you see a tiger, they said don't run, just stare at it and it will back off. The seventeen kilometres seemed like a long trek, but we were eager and having now been fed and clothed felt somewhat revitalized.

It must have been past midday when we reached Loebeck Linggau, and looked in vain for a massive Allied force.

Instead, we were directed to a neat but small wooden house with the four flags of Britain, America, Holland and China fluttering above it. Inside were four soldiers: Corps Officer Wilhelm, Regimental Sergeant-Major Hakkenberg, Sergeant van Hasselt and Chinese officer Suet. They all welcomed us warmly.

But where was the massive Allied force sent to Sumatra, one of the world's largest islands, to enforce the surrender of the Japanese and ensure the safety and liberation of all of their prisoners?

To our utter astonishment, we were told that we were looking at a fifth of it. Only twenty-one Allied soldiers — including three Hollanders and one Chinese — had so far arrived on the island. But under the inspired leadership of Major Gideon Jacobs, a young South African Royal Marine, they were already making their presence felt.

With atom bombs ready to drop and an anticipated Japanese surrender in sight, Major Jacobs had been parachuted into the jungle in the north of Sumatra accompanied by two Australians, Sergeants Gillam and Bates, an Indonesian-Chinese called Tjoeng and Sergeant 'Happy' Plessman, a Hollander, who had served in the Dutch Resistance during the war in Europe. On the day that Japanese Emperor Hirohito told his people that they had to think the unthinkable — that the war with the Allies had ended in their abject defeat — Major Jacobs led his tiny force into Medan, where he established his headquarters and contacted an astonished Japanese Commanding General, not knowing what kind of reception he was going to receive.

It was not exactly friendly — on either side — but it seemed to be formally correct, and Jacobs set to work. In short order they located what the Japanese said were all the Prisoner of War and the Civilian Internment Camps on the island and radioed Lord Mountbatten's SEAC Headquarters at Kandy, in Ceylon, for more parachutists to be dropped to take control of strategic centres.

In all, four more groups, each comprising four men, were dropped in immediate response — one of them the group we encountered that day at Loebok Linggau.

More troops were to follow, some by air from Singapore, and other, larger, reinforcements by sea. Meantime, the four-man units under Major Jacobs' direction soldiered on.

Today, the rescue of the prisoners of war and the internees would have taken a fortnight or more to arrange and another month to implement. Back in 1945 a couple of handfuls of very young men made all the difference between life and death to thousands.

After his preliminary tour of inspection, Major Jacobs still had no knowledge of our own camp, tucked away on the west coast. It was only after he visited the Prisoner of War Camp at Palembang that he became suspicious. There, each of the servicemen was asked to write a report of his experiences and two of these particularly attracted his attention.

Shipwreck survivor Robert Seddon, a Royal Marine, was struggling to reach the shore of Bangka Island at a most inappropriate time. He crawled onto the beach straight into the midst of the Bangka massacre and was stabbed and left for dead. He saw the other bodies littering the beach.

Stoker Lloyd, of the Royal Navy, was the eye-witness who escaped being killed on the beach by holding his breath and swimming under water. Some of the machinegun bullets grazed him, but he was not seriously injured and managed to swim away. Captured later, he was held with other prisoners at Muntok before being transferred to Palembang. It was as a result of reading the reports of these two men that Major Jacobs realized that a number of civilian internees had not been accounted for. He knew then that there must be another two camps on the island, separately housing women and men.

The Japanese were extremely reluctant to talk about them — perhaps because the camps held survivors of the *Vyner Brooke* who could provide numbers and personal details of those Australian nurses who should have been protected by the bold Red Cross that they wore on their breast, but who, instead, had been so brutishly slaughtered. In any event, they gave evasive answers to Major Jacobs' questions. It was only after considerable and persistent pressure had been applied that they finally revealed that the hidden camps were at Loebock Linggau.

We found the story enthralling, and the soldiers gave us tea, soft drinks and cakes as they answered our questions. We asked how far the Japanese had advanced and were told to the borders of India at Kohima and Imphal, but not into India itself.

"What about Australia?"

"They got close. Down to New Guinea and the Solomon Islands, but no further. And they couldn't get to Hawaii, either."

Some unfamiliar words, such as 'Jeep' and 'Penicillin' were mentioned. Then it was time to start on our return journey.

We thanked them and told them how glad everyone was that they had arrived, and made our way out of the town for the long trek back to our camp.

It was already afternoon by now, and while we were trudging back along the dirt road, it got dark. Only the lights of the stars were there to guide us. In that almost total darkness, they were very bright, they were beautiful and special.

There were now all sorts of weird noises coming from the forest. "What are you going to do if you meet a tiger now?" said one of the boys. "Stare at it," was the answer. "How are you going to see his eyes in the dark?" "Don't worry, a tiger is like a cat. Its eyes glow in the dark."

Fortunately, we did not come upon any tiger and got back to the camp safely. I thought Marc was asleep so I flopped down.

"What was the headquarters like?" Marc was not asleep. I recounted the whole story to him about the trek, the hut with its flags, and the weird noises of the jungle at night. Then I told him about Major Jacobs and we both had another titbit from the tin on the shelf and then went to sleep.

Soon it was our turn to be airlifted out. It must have been September 1945. I took Marc with me to go and say goodbye to the priests and Brothers. There was talk that we had to forgive our enemies, pray for Captain Seki and the rest of our captors.

Possibly I could have done that for the little Civilian Commandant who had given flowers for the funerals, but I could not bring myself to do it for Seki, a feeling obviously with some foundation, for some months later Seki was sentenced to fifteen years imprisonment by the War Crimes Tribunal.

We said, "Goodbye, our turn has come to be airlifted out," and someone said, "May the Lord go with you," or words to that effect. Instinctively I replied in Latin "*Et cum spiritu tuo.*" They all laughed.

Someone called, "Hurry up!" so with our little bundles of personal possessions Marc and I ran to the waiting lorries. They were now being driven by British and Dutch personnel instead of Japanese, although the Japanese had been retained to maintain law and order around the area.

The airfield was at Lahat, a bigger town about one hundred miles away. We were to get there by train. We got into the trucks and were driven to the Railway Station at Loebok Linggau. There we entrained for the longer journey to Lahat. Along the way we saw columns of Japanese soldiers. It was amazing to see all these thousands of soldiers obeying the orders of Major Jacobs and his four companions. The Japanese certainly had discipline and gave unquestioning obedience to orders from authority. They seemed to have gone into complete reverse, and they were now bowing to us and carrying our baggage.

The train journey was quite pleasant, although a bit slow. The surrounding countryside had a certain beauty of its own. I remember thinking, 'How vast the jungle is here, compared to Malaya.'

At the airfield at Lahat, we got into a Dakota DC 4 army plane. The seats were like those in an old style bus — just benches along each side of the passageway, with passengers facing each other. The benches were bolted to the floor. As far as I can remember, when the plane took off, we had to hang on to something to keep ourselves steady.

The windows had stoppers in their centres — just like bathtub rubber plugs with chains, only larger. The stoppers were about four inches in diameter and one could pull them out and put them back whereupon they fitted tightly by suction.

We amused ourselves by pulling them out and holding empty sweet wrappers or other disposables near them, and watching these sucked out. It was also cooler when the stoppers were out.

Approaching Singapore, we saw a large fleet of British warships in the harbour together with some ships of the Allied navies. It was really a magnificent and heart-warming sight, and brought a tear to my eye.

When we arrived in Singapore we were taken to the British Military Hospital at Alexandra. There, all of our personal details were recorded and I enquired about my father. They did not know where he was, nor even if he was alive or dead. But they said they would ask the Red Cross to try to find him.

We stayed there for over a week for detoxification and to get all the bugs out of us. We were given so much Mepacrine and Atabrine to get rid of the malaria bug that our skin became yellow.

Whilst in the Hospital we got the SEAC newspapers and some snippets of information from both the civilian and uniformed personnel with whom we came into contact. We had hundreds of questions and couldn't wait to find out what had happened. It must be remembered that we had been cut off from all news for the entire duration of our internment — three and a half years. Things had changed tremendously in that time. Churchill and Roosevelt were no longer the leaders. There were new names now: Truman in America and Attlee in England.

We saw Jeeps and heard about DUKWs — simply called 'Ducks' — the new amphibious landing craft which had been invented to carry the troops right up the beaches and keep on going on dry land.

New medicines had been discovered: Penicillin, Mepacrine and Atabrine and little tablets for water purification which, when dropped into a bucket of water, however stale, could eliminate all germs and make it drinkable.

We heard about D-Day in Europe, and the battles from island to island across the Pacific right to Iwojima on the doorstep of Japan. And then of course the Atom Bombs which ended the war in two swift blows.

Most interesting to us was the progress of Mountbatten's forces fighting their way through the monsoon-drenched jungles of Burma, and retaking Rangoon.

In August 1943, at the Quebec Conference, Winston Churchill and President Roosevelt had agreed that American General Douglas MacArthur should remain the Supreme Commander of Allied Forces in the South-West Pacific and that Lord Louis Mountbatten should be appointed Supreme Commander in South-East Asia with headquarters in India and an American deputy.

Mountbatten saw the liberation of Burma, long wholly occupied by the Japanese, as a major concern.

However, at Quebec it had also been agreed by the Allies that the defeat of Germany must take precedence over the defeat of Japan and men and munitions of war were allocated accordingly. General William Slim's 'Forgotten' 14th Army in India did not have the means to make a realistic attempt to actually drive the Japanese out of Burma, but Major-General Orde Wingate and the three thousand British and Gurkha members of the 7th Indian Brigade — known as 'The Chindits' — crossed the River Chindwin into Burma in February 1943 and, continuously re-supplied from the air, advanced over five hundred miles behind enemy lines, through malarial swamp and snake-infested jungle, blowing up railways ambushing Japanese units, killing the enemy wherever encountered. A second foray across the Chindwin by the Chindits was even more successful, but a major British campaign to liberate Burma was still some way off when the Japanese themselves sowed the seeds of their own abject defeat.

Architect of Victory in South-East Asia
Admiral Lord Louis Mountbatten
Supreme Allied Commander SEAC
with his wife, Lady Edwina

In a massive surprise assault in March 1944 they attacked the mountainous British positions at Imphal, a small town which, with neighbouring Kohima, guarded 'the gateway to India'. At Imphal, the garrison, supplied by air, held their positions for three months against wave after wave of attacks by an ever more savage and desperate enemy. When they were finally relieved and the siege of the town was lifted, thirteen thousand Japanese soldiers lay dead.

At Kohima, Japanese paratroops spearheaded a similarly massive assault on a garrison of only one hundred and fifty. Grotesquely outnumbered in fighting fearsome in its ferocity and under continuous bombardment by two hundred and fifty guns which the enemy had dragged up to the battle through the mud and the jungles of Burma, the tiny garrison held on to as much of the town as it could until relieved by superior forces two and a half weeks later. But the battle didn't end there. It raged for another two and a half months, during which time RAF bombers, flying from airfields in Assam, attacked the enemy day and night in more than two thousand sorties before the Japanese called a retreat.

At Kohima they suffered the greatest military defeat in all of their history. Five Japanese divisions were wholly destroyed. They lost fifty-three thousand men and all of their artillery. The 14th Army suffered sixteen thousand seven hundred casualties, but not a gun was lost, nor an inch of ground, either. The battle of Kohima marked an end to Japan's dream of the subjugation of all of the peoples of South-East Asia. It was a clearly defined turning-point immortalised in the inscription on the Kohima memorial to all of those men from the forces of the Empire who died there:

When you go home, tell them of us, and say
"For your tomorrow we gave our today"

Now the 14th Army began the long and arduous task of following up the victory and liberating Burma. It was to take almost a year.

British and Imperial forces, Indian and African, assisted

by Indian elephants, fought their way through the monsoonal, muddy jungle; the elephants being employed to uproot trees to bridge streams and rivers for vehicles to cross. Desert General Masservy, who had done well against the Italians in North Africa, was one of many new commanders brought in to engage in a totally different kind of war to that which he had fought in the desert. There it had been a war of movement. Here, every inch was hard fought and progress reduced to a snail's pace.

General Masservy recommended that Sherman tanks be brought in. Unheard of in the steamy Burmese jungles, though inferior in Europe to German armour, they were ideal for use in Burma, big enough to go over the mud and hit Japanese strongpoints with devastating effect.

In August 1944, the Allied armies — British divisions, American regiments and the Chinese 22nd division met at a place called Bhamo, and from then on it was only a matter of time before Rangoon, the Burmese capital, was liberated, the Burma Road was reopened and oil supples resumed through the little-known man-made wonder, the incredible 2,200-mile pipeline from Calcutta to Kunming.

Rangoon was retaken in May 1945 by a two-pronged attack, Operation Dracula, which only a year before had been thought impossible to mount before October/November. It involved sea-borne invasion together with an assault by General Masservy's Division from the north. The Japanese withdrew hurriedly before the 14th Army arrived, after donating arms, ammunition — and even field guns — to local bands of *dacoits*, Burmese bandits, to hinder the British advance.

Nevertheless, as law-abiding Burmese welcomed their liberators, and the whole of the country was rapidly secured and Mountbatten transferred his headquarters to Kandy, the ancient capital of Ceylon, there to formulate plans for the liberation of the rest of South-East Asia and all the prisoners, service and civilian, held there by the Japanese.

Although we did not know it at the time, it was these plans, formulated in Kandy, which led to our own safe release from Japanese captivity in Sumatra.

Lord Louis Mountbatten and his staff planned well. It is no exaggeration to say that we owe them our lives.

We learned that Lady Mountbatten who was the head of the St John's Ambulance Brigade, had a lot to do with the smooth return of the prisoners.

While we were preparing to leave Belalau, we were unaware of the fact that she had arrived in Sumatra and spent a week there, mostly in Palembang. The enlisted men in the Army camps she visited were simply overwhelming in their praise of her. She was an inspiration to them and I did not hear a single man who did not agree that she was wonderful.

She was not a large person, in fact almost frail, but her energy, determination and strength of character was unmistakeable. Continually out and about on active tours of inspection, she was sunburned golden brown. When she met the Japanese commandant of the camp in Palembang she told him to 'get out of her sight.' Everybody got to know of her and, when she came by, there was always a ripple of excitement in the ranks.

We were then sent to Raffles Hotel. The famous hotel had been requisitioned for use as a Transit Camp for homeward-bound ex-prisoners of war and internees and we were sent there with the aim of eventual onward passage to England.

Although it was functioning as a transit camp, it was still run as a world-class hotel with all the liveried staff, glittering cutlery and superb service. It was wonderful. In the tearoom, the Supreme Allied Commander in South-East, Lord Louis Mountbatten came to see us and gave a speech.

My first impression of him was a good one. He was dressed in a crisp white Admiral's uniform, and his bearing was tall and straight. He spoke clearly and succinctly. After greeting us, he said that there had been plans for a large invasion force to liberate Singapore and Malaya. The fact that the Japanese Army had obeyed the surrender instructions from Tokyo had obviated that necessity, and made the transfer of power clean and smooth.

In Europe, he said, some of those liberated had taken revenge. Germans had been beaten up, even murdered. Lord Louis said he did not like what he saw there. We had fought the war to stop the enemy's atrocities and crimes against humanity. If we did the same things, he said, we would be as bad as our enemies.

A War Crimes Commission had been established and we were assured that any Japanese who had committed a War Crime would pay for it. "Leave it to us," he said, "We will not let anyone get away.

"Another thing," he said, "you should not judge a person until you have checked into the matter yourself." In the course of his investigations, he said that he had many times had to interview an accused person and come away very surprised when the true facts were revealed.

"So try to forget about the whole horrible episode. Think of it as a bad nightmare. You have all you need now and your freedom. Go out and enjoy yourselves and leave it to us to deal with the enemy."

I think Lady Mountbatten was there too, but cannot remember for sure. After the speech Lord Mountbatten came around and shook hands with each and every one of us.

The speech seemed to satisfy everybody. Afterwards it was announced that there would be a ball in the hotel at the weekend.

At dinner I remember trying to guide Marc as to which knives and forks he should use. The soup spoon was not much of a problem, but where some of the other cutlery was concerned, he needed a bit of guidance. Unlike the old days, nobody seemed to bother too much with etiquette so we all just enjoyed ourselves.

We were given new clothes, and a weekly spending allowance of five pounds. (At that time the exchange rate was about one pound sterling to eight dollars fifty Straits dollars).

The night for the ball came. The lads were to go in the jungle green uniforms which had been provided by the RAPWI (Repatriation of Allied Prisoners of War and Internees) organization and the girls and ladies could choose either to go in uniform or put on what civilian dresses they still had. At the ball there were some very beautiful girls — and one in particular, who remains vividly in my memory as the most beautiful girl I have ever seen.

She had golden hair, exquisitely cut features, and blue-green eyes. Amongst all the other girls in the room, she stood out for her remarkable looks, her charm and laughter. She was truly the fairest of them all and reminded me of the song *Like a Golden Dream* . . .

There was a man at her side and, to my amazement, they made their way to our table and asked if they could join us. Only my friend and I were sitting at the table and, of course, we quickly said "Certainly!"

It transpired that the man at her side was her brother. Her father was Scottish and her mother French, and that she had been born in Indo-China. She spoke with a slight French accent, but, unlike some French girls, not overwhelmingly so.

After some talk about the war and the search for missing family and loved ones, she suddenly asked me to dance. I was absolutely flabbergasted. I couldn't believe this was really happening. It must be part of a dream. Was I back at the swamp, hallucinating again? Then I saw that it was really so. She reached out and held my right hand as we stood up together to walk out onto the floor.

But I had no idea at all of how to dance, I fumbled and stuttered not knowing what to do. I wanted to hold her and dance with her. Oh, how I wanted to! But I was afraid of making a fool of myself on the dance floor. I found I was sinking back into my chair like a lump of lead.

She sat back again, and resumed the small talk. Her brother was smiling, amused, it seemed. Then after a while, another young man in jungle green came up and asked her whether she would like to dance. And she accepted. The band was playing a waltz.

After the dance they returned to our table where her dancing partner now stuck around like a leech, inviting his obnoxious self to our table, never leaving her side. When the evening ended and we went back to our rooms, the words of

131

another tune came to mind, *After the Ball Was Over* . . .

I sprawled on the sheets. That night I did not sleep like a log, I slept fitfully, uneasily, and woke unrefreshed.

In the morning when I went down to breakfast I met the friend who had shared my table. He said, "Why did you do that? She was the loveliest girl in the room. Why did you let that chap muscle in?" I sighed. "It just happened."

He shook his head in despair.

After the ball, Marc and I and three other boys went around everywhere together. We went along Beach Road, looked at the shops and bargained with the hawkers. We went to the Forces' Clubs, wandered through Chinatown and, generally took Mountbatten's advice and did our best to put our horrific experiences behind us and really enjoy ourselves.

And, of course, after many a long year, we went to the cinema.

The *Alhambra* was fairly close to Raffles Hotel, and the *Capitol* and *Cathay* cinemas in the city centre. Further out were the three massive amusement parks, *The Great World, The Happy World* and *The New World*, ablaze with Chinese lanterns and coloured lights.

The Great World was the nearest to the hotel, so that was the one we sampled first. It had lots of rides and they were great. It had a Crazy House with moving floors; wayside Chinese or Malay operas; puppet shows; shooting galleries and shops of all kinds selling fantastically embroidered silks, 'Ronson' lighters (made in local workshops) and 'genuine Swiss watches' (made who knows where.) The *Worlds* of Singapore at this time were packed with men of all nations seeking instant 'fruits of the peace', a release from the fear and tensions of a long war in which they had seen many friends die.

Some found it on a dance floor, in the arms of a taxidance hostess, paid to dance with you — for the whole evening if you could afford to invest in a roll of tickets at twenty-five cents a dance. But come *God Save the King,* a polite *amah* or mother would usually appear out of nowhere and whisk her away from her disappointed partner to disappear into the night in a home-bound rickshaw. Needless to say, such forbidden fruits and disappointments were not what we boys were looking for. We enjoyed the rides and the freewheeling atmosphere of fun and, at all these *Worlds*, Marc could come with us at any time, day or night.

But he was barred entry to the Forces' Clubs in the evening because of his age. Which was just as well. For in them, as the evenings wore on, minor disputes exploded into fights. It was either the Yanks and the British, or the British and the Australians, or the Navy and the Army or something else. In their cups — *anything* else. A slight or throwaway remark was all that it needed.

We learned to position ourselves near a door. When the fight started we would move off quietly. The drinks had to be paid for before you got them so there was no delay there. Sometimes we really had to leave in quite a hurry. We were outside in a flash, while the confusion reigned, with red-capped Military Police blowing their whistles as the unruly were taken away.

We did not smoke, so when our money ran out we found that we could get extra by selling our cigarette ration to street vendors. Enough to go to the movies.

Marc and I were scheduled to fly out to England. Now our number came up. The following week we would be leaving Singapore for the UK. We collected all the documents we needed for our departure and wondered about extra clothes. "What will England be like?" we asked. "Cold, damned cold," was the reply.

Then fate again intervened. A lady officer in Red Cross uniform came to see us, to tell us that my father had been traced. He had been hidden by a Chinese *baba* family for the duration of the war, and not harmed. We were asked to make a decision. Marc and I could still get free passage to England should we wish it, but dad unfortunately could not. He would have had to pay the full fare.

As we had lost nearly everything in the war, except a few personal belongings, there was very little hope of scraping up the money for his fare. One idea put forward was for us two to go to England first, establish ourselves, and then send for my father. We thought about it long and hard, but to go now, so soon after we had been re-united, would have broken Dad's heart. So we decided to stay.

The Red Cross had already told my father of the fate of his wife and of his daughters Grace and Dix, so when Marc and I went to the place where he was staying and threw our arms round him he was overjoyed. We couldn't stop hugging each other and we all cried a bit.

At last we were together again.

The war was truly over.

12 September 1945
THE JAPANESE SURRENDER SINGAPORE
Above: Lord Louis Mountbatten,
Supreme Allied Commander S.E.Asia, enters the city
Facing, top: He inspects Australian troops
Facing, bottom: In front of the Municipal Buildings,
he takes the salute at the Victory Parade

Myself at Fort Canning

Sequel

WITH PEACE AND THE GRADUAL RETURN of normality, I resumed and completed my education and, for some years, I worked at Fort Canning, in Singapore. One day, years later, I walked down to the City to look at the shops. In Battery Road, about midway between the General Post Office and Raffles Place, on the opposite side to the GH Cafe, there was a large bookstore.

I wandered in and was standing, looking down at some books in the centre low stands. There was another man beside me, also browsing. There was something familiar about his stance as I turned and looked.

It was James Reid. He said, "Good Lord, is it you!"

We asked each other how we were, and evoked some war memories, then the conversation turned to the war games we had in the Internment Camp at Irenelaan in Palembang.

He said, "You nearly won, you know."

I nodded.

He said, "You don't know how close your team came to winning."

I thought back in my mind.

"I gathered that, from the position we had advanced to," I told him. "But didn't say anything at the time."

"You hardly had the opportunity," he said. "How was your eye? Was it very painful?"

"Very," I said. "At least until I got to the hospital and they gave me an injection."

"And how is it now?"

"I can see quite well, actually. But Doctor Goldberg warned me at the time that I might need an operation when I'm about fifty."

"I hope not." he said. "But at least that's still some way off."

"Yes."

We shared some more memories, then "Wasn't it great the way the Japs were defeated?" he said. "How suddenly it all happened! Who do you think did the most to save us? MacArthur or Mountbatten?"

"No question," I said. "It must be Mountbatten. He is the one who saved us."

And I am just as sure of it today.

Armoured Cars inside Fort Canning

Inside Fort Canning
Top: Inspection Parade
Bottom: Myself and Armoured Car

Appendix

From *The Sarawak Gazette,* November 1927

ss Vyner Brooke

We understand that the new steamer for the Sarawak Steamship Co Ltd is being launched by Her Highness The Ranee at Leith on 10th November 1927. The following is a brief description of the ship:

Builders Messrs Ramage and Ferguson of Leith

	Hull
Length overall	251ft
Breadth	41ft
Moulded depth	17ft
Maximum draught	16ft
Speed	12 – 13 knots
Economic speed	11 – 12 knots
Engine	Twin Screw
Cylinders	6 of 16,27 and 44in diameter in each pair
Boilers	2 single ended by Barclay, Curle & Co
Working pressure	180lbs

She is designed with a straight stem and round stern. Her bows are well flared. She is fitted with 10in. bilge keels and is schooner rigged. She is being built to Lloyds classification 100 A1. All steel is British. She has six watertight bulkheads so arranged that a double bottom is unnecessary.

She is flush decked with tween decks. All decks are steel sheathed with 2½in. teak. Height between all decks 7ft 6in.

The main deck has been kept as clear as possible of all houses to leave ample space for deck passengers.

Accommodation on this deck is provided for crew situated forward and clerks, stewards, boys, etc., aft. On this deck is situated the refrigerating machinery with a cold store room designed for temperatures to be maintained at 2 degrees below freezing point.

On the upper deck cabin-deck accommodation is provided for 44 first class passengers situated amidships. At the forward end of this accommodation is a large Saloon 40ft by 24ft. All tables are folding so as to allow for ample space if there are not a full complement of first class passengers. Dining tables are all separate, each table seating four persons.

This saloon is panelled to the full height with polished mahogany and is provided with 20 large windows of 'Laycock' type, these are easily opened and locked at any height to suit the convenience of passengers. All furniture is of mahogany, the chairs being of Chippendale design with leather seats. The seats are reversible and have cane on the underside. In the saloon are two houses containing a pantry and a bar.

The saloon is lighted by means of ten ceiling lights, having cut crystal bowls, it is ventilated by means of 6 ceiling fans of 30in. diameter. Further individual lighting is provided by mean of polished brass standards with silk shades at each table. There are, aft of the saloon, 6 cabins 4 of 2 berths each and 2 of 3 berths. Entrance to these is directly from the after end of the saloon. Amidships are situated 2 bathrooms and 2 lavatories. The passageway leading to these cabins is panelled on both sides and has a mahogany dado round the boiler casing. All this accommodation is insulated.

Situated aft of the engine room casing are 8 4-berth staterooms with 5 bathrooms and 4 lavatories. The upper bunks in this accommodation are folding thus leaving ample space when used by 2 passengers only.

All cabins are fitted with washbasins and water is laid on direct, also all waste pipes lead to the sea. The bathrooms and lavatories are white tiled throughout. Bathrooms are fitted with 12in. bracket fans and lavatories are ventilated by means of exhaust fans.

A handsome staircase leads from the after end of the saloon to the shade deck. On this deck are situated the cabins de luxe. Special attention has been given to these cabins; they are panelled throughout with mahogany and maple and are carpeted; all furniture is leather covered and fittings are of bronze. These two special cabins are furnished with brass bedsteads. A comfortable private sitting room is also provided for use of passengers using this suite. Aft of this accommodation is ample deck space providing room for two games of deck quoits and deck tennis for those who need exercise. It is intended to furnish the after end of the shade deck with rattan furniture thus making a comfortable verandah for use of passengers. Access to this verandah is obtained by means of ladders on either side leading from the upper deck.

As regards cargo, large hatches have been provided and at each hatch are placed 2 cranes each designed to lift 3 tons. This should ensure speedy handling of cargo. A 'heavy derrick' with winch is also provided, designed to lift 20 tons. This is a considerable advancement on the lifting capacity of the present steamers engaged in this trade.

The vessel is fitted with wireless and has a full supply of lifeboats, rafts and lifebelts for 650 persons.

Courtesy Jabatan Muzium Sarawak
(Sarawak Museum Department),
Sarawak, Malaysia

Select Bibliography

Graham Chisholm — *The Days Were Like Years*
and the Years Were Long

Winston S. Churchill — *The Second World War*

Stanley Davidson — *The Principles and Practice of Medicine*

Penrod Dean — *Singapore Samurai*

N.I. Low — *When Singapore Was Syonan-to*

Galley Press — *2194 Days of War*

Shirley Fenton Howe — *The Forgotten Ones*

G.F. Jacobs — *Prelude to the Monsoon*

Catherine Kenny — *The Captives*

B.H. Liddell Hart — *History of the Second World War*

James Lunt — *A Hell of a Licking: The Retreat from Burma*

William McDougall, Jnr — *By Eastern Windows*

Readers Digest — *Illustrated Story of World War II*

Rohan D Rivett — *Behind Bamboo*

Lord Russell of Liverpool — *Knights of Bushido*

The Times of Singapore — *Fortress Singapore*

Tsuji — *Japan's Greatest Victory, Britain's Greatest Defeat*

Lavinia Warner and John Sandilands — *Women Beyond the Wire*